¡FEMINISMO!

¡FEMINISMO!

The Woman's Movement in Argentina
From Its Beginnings to Eva Perón

By Marifran Carlson

Introduction by George I. Blanksten

ACADEMY
CHICAGO

I dedicate this book to Alicia Moreau de Justo, for her feminist militancy and because she was a relentless champion of political freedom and social justice in Argentina and throughout the world.

Published in 1988 by

Academy Chicago Publishers
213 West Institute Place
Chicago, Illinois 60610

Library of Congress Cataloging-in-Publication Data

Carlson, Marifran, 1942–
    Feminismo.

      Bibliography: p. 209
      1. Feminism—Argentina—History.   2. Women social reformers—Argentina—History—Argentina—History—19th century.   3. Feminists—Argentina—History.
I. Title.
HQ1533.C28   1987   305.4'2'0982   85-18567
ISBN 0-89733-152-4
ISBN 0-89733-168-0 (pbk.)

Acknowledgements

I am grateful to the Latin American Studies Department at the University of Chicago for providing me with a research grant to travel to Buenos Aires, Argentina in 1976 and 1977; also to my dissertation committee, T. Bentley Duncan, John Coatsworth, and Freidrich Katz for their support. I want to thank my fellow pioneers in the field of Argentine women's history: Cynthia Little, Sandra McGee Deutsch, Marysa Navarro, Asunción Lavrin, Nancy Hollander, and Donna Guy. Thanks also to Anita Miller at Academy Chicago Publishers for her careful editing of the revised manuscript.

Many people in Buenos Aires helped me with my research. Among them were Jorgelina Lozada, Elena Bergman, Gainza Paz, Mary Feijoó, Theresa Blaksley, Enrique Callejón, Eva Clementi, Blanca Stabile, Nidia Winograd, and Estella Erasquín de Cordero. The library staffs at the Asociación Cristiana Femenina, the Consejo Nacional de Mujeres, the Biblioteca Juan B. Justo, *La Prensa*, the Biblioteca Nacional, and the Archivo General de la Nación were also very helpful.

My special thanks to Alicia Moreau de Justo who was one of the founders and the greatest leader of Argentine feminism. In 1977 she invited me to her home where I conducted a series of interviews. Despite her advanced age, (she was ninety-two at the time), she was able to remember important details and events of the feminist movement.

Moreau's personal strength, warmth, kindness, and courage inspired me to continue with the task of writing the history of the Argentine feminists. On October 11, 1985, Alicia Moreau celebrated her one hundreth birthday. Unfortunately I was not able to attend the many celebrations that paid homage to this extraordinary woman. Argentina's first female medical doctor, she was also a journalist, educator, politician and strong defender of human rights. From 1978 to 1986 Dr. Moreau served as co-director with President Raúl Alfonsín on the Argentine Committee of Human Rights. Alicia Moreau died in May of 1986, just a few months before her one hundred and first birthday.

CONTENTS

Introduction

In this volume Marifran Carlson provides us with a pioneering history of the feminist movement in Argentina. The book takes us from the early participation of women of that country's upper class in the charitable work of the Argentine Beneficent Society, through the dedicated contribution of that nation's women to the development of what has long been regarded as the best system of national education in all of Latin America, through the involvement of Argentine women in the free-thought and Socialist movements, both considered radical in nineteenth-century Spanish America, into the twentieth century, and — finally — the politicization of the nation's women during the Perón period.

The story, as told in the following pages, is remarkable in a number of senses. For one thing, this is a species of intellectual history, pausing along the way to examine the writings and the ideas of the Argentines who were especially influential in the development of the feminist movement. Thus we have in this book a rare opportunity to become acquainted intellectually with such towering Argentine figures as Bernardino Rivadavia, the country's first President; Domingo Faustino Sarmiento, the nation's celebrated "schoolmaster-President;" Dr Cecilia Grierson, Argentina's first female physician and an early feminist; Sara Justo, the crusading Socialist who founded the Association of Argentine University Women; and even with Maria Eva ("Evita") Duarte de Perón, who at last brought woman suffrage to Argentina.

Also striking, in this account, is the dramatic speed with which the social and political roles of women have changed in Argentina. The often tumultuous road from chattel to politicized voter has been travelled in that country in the space of one and one-half centuries. This is an experience standing in sharp contrast to the longer and slower rates of social change in the older societies of Western Europe, especially of Spain, to which Argentina traces its cultural origins. The women of Argentina still face a significant distance to be travelled, to be sure; but this should not detract from the impressive time frame of the changes recorded in this book.

But perhaps most remarkably of all, this history of the feminist movement illustrates a curious Argentine characteristic often noted in other areas of change in that country. That characteristic is paradox or apparent contradiction. The role of women has moved and changed within the context of three paradoxes, each dramatically and notably Argentine.

The first is what Sarmiento himself, who should have known better, called the conflict between civilization and barbarism. Even in colonial times what is now Argentina was the most Europeanized or Westernized part of Spanish America. Little in the way of indigenous American Indian culture existed to retard the Westernization of Argentina. Indeed the country strikes the foreign observer as being more European than South American, and has received more immigrants from Europe than any other American republic with the sole exception of the United States .

Yet at the beginning of the twentieth century, most of the people of Argentina, as "civilized" as that country was, were illiterate. In 1869 the nation's first census reported 25.2% of the male population, and only 18.3% of the females, to be literate. By 1895 these data had advanced to 49.2% for men and 41.5% for women. If these figures reflect a disadvantaged base from which a feminist movement might be launched, it should be remembered that this was the most Europeanized or Westernized — "civilized," if you will — place to be found anywhere in all of Spanish America.

Secondly, during much of the nineteenth century, and even the twentieth, Argentine society and politics were severely polarized. *Machismo*, the glorification of male virtues, dominated the scene, and "uncivilized barbarians" were often in power. Forty-three newspapers were published in Argentina when Juan Manuel de Rosas came to power at the dawn of the 1830s. These were reduced to fifteen in 1834 and were only three in 1835. "Why would Rosas want newspapers?" an observer once asked.

Nevertheless, in those same nineteenth and twentieth centuries that same Argentina was blessed by the talents of a number of remarkably liberated and far-sighted leaders. There was President Rivadavia, who founded the Beneficent Society, the cradle of a wide range of Argentine women's activities. "It is eminently useful and just to give serious attention to the education of women," he said, "to the improvement of their customs and the means through which they achieve their basic necessities, so that we may pass laws which establish their rights and responsibilities and assure them the happiness which they deserve."

And there was Sarmiento, the creator of a national system of education which was directed in major measure to the participation of females as teachers and as learners. "The separation of the sexes in different schools derives from the . . . source which prevents women from participating in public acts," he once said. "The cumulative result is . . . that a woman does not dare to show herself to be intelligent . . . Such are our customs, the remnants of barbarism . . ."

Ironically, it remained for the twentieth century to present Argentine feminism with its most maddening of paradoxes. Woman suffrage and the transformation of Argentine women into a mass of actors on the national political scene became facts through the work of Juan and Eva Perón. The latter, perhaps inevitably a controversial figure, was widely rejected and even hated by the pre-*Peronista* leadership of the Argentine feminist movement. As *Peronismo* stole the direction of the labor movement from the Socialist and Radical parties, so Eva Perón wrenched the helm of Argentine feminism from the hands of its earlier stewards.

Essentially, there were two reasons, one social and the other ideological, for the antagonism between *Peronismo* and the traditional leadership of Argentine feminism. The first was that in pre-*Peronista* times the women's movement had been dominated by pioneers. They were the first women to be educated, the first to receive doctors' degrees, the first to enter the professions. As radical and as threatening as they might have seemed to the male population, the early feminist pioneers were leaders. As such they represented an elite. Although some had been in the free-thought and Socialist movements, many of the pre-*Peronista* feminists had been identified with the "Oligarchy" and the landowning upper class.

Eva Perón, on the other hand, reached out to the underprivileged, to Argentina's lower classes, to the mass of women who were followers rather than to the minority who had been leaders. "Because I have seen that women never have had material or spiritual opportunities — only poetry took them into account—and because I have known that women were a moral and spiritual resource of the world, I have placed myself at the side of all women of my country," Evita said, "to struggle resolutely with them not only for the vindication of ourselves but also of our homes, our children, and our husbands." The social division between *Peronista* feminism and its predecessor was thus the formidable gap between the leadership elite and the downtrodden of the lower classes.

The ideological division was also great. Notwithstanding substantial assistance from a number of enlightened males — again, the names of Rivadavia and Sarmiento come to mind — pre-*Peronista* feminism was essentially of, by, and for Argentine women, whatever their ideological stripe. This differed widely from the view brought by Evita. *Peronismo* was associated, especially in the 1940s and 1950s, with the dictatorship of a *man*, Juan Domingo Perón, regarded by his followers and collaborators, including Evita, as virtually infallible. Pre-*Peronista* feminism could never be brought to accept the infallibility of Perón or any other man. Yet this was precisely what Evita demanded. She asserted that it was the historic role of women to follow great men. "For a woman to be a *Peronista*," she said, "is before anything to be loyal to Perón, subordinate to Perón, and to have blind confidence in Perón."

To expect pre-*Peronista* feminism to embrace such a commitment would be to expect the impossible. Perhaps ironically, this is the central reason that traditional feminism now appears to have lost the day in Argentina. Contemporary feminism in that country now marches to the drum of *Peronismo*. It is the movement of the downtrodden, the lower classes; it has turned its back on the teachings of the great leaders of the nineteenth and twentieth centuries, whose story is told in the following pages.

Marifran Carlson has traced the difficult course of Argentine feminism, examining its achievements, its struggles, and its paradoxes. It is sometimes said that only a hardy crop can survive in a rocky soil. In reading this book, one is helped to form a judgment on whether this will in the long run be true of the struggle of Argentine women for recognition and self-realization.

George I. Blanksten
Northwestern University
Evanston, Illinois

1

The Background:
Colonialism and Independence

When Spain established her American colonies in the late
fifteenth and early sixteenth centuries, she was an important European power not yet consolidated into a nation.
Spain was, in fact, a loose confederation of warring kingdoms before the marriage, in 1469, of Isabella of Castile
and Ferdinand of Aragon, who strengthened the central
authority of the Crown by controlling the rebellious aristocracy and negotiating agreements with the Church. In 1492
the kingdoms of Castile and Aragon united to evict the
Moors from Granada; these wars against the Moorish in-
fidels brought the masses and the nobles together in religious patriotism. Isabella became the patroness of the
Holy Inquisition, zealously working to convert or expel
Jews and Moslems from Spain and to convert the infidel
outside Spain. Only a few months after the reconquest of
Granada, the Pope, Alexander VI, who was himself Spanish, gave approval to the Spanish monarchs to explore the
unknown reaches of the world, both to bring Christ to whatever peoples dwelt there and to use the spices and precious
metals, which were doubtless also to be found there, to re-
plenish the Spanish treasury from the depredations of
eight centuries of holy wars.

A series of papal bulls and treaties divided the New
World between Spain and Portugal. In 1494, for example,
the Treaty of Tordesillas gave Spain power over the New
World, with the exception of the territory that is now Brazil,

which was ceded to Portugal. Conquest of these lands, completed by the *conquistadores* within fifty years of the New World's discovery by Columbus, was followed by a protracted period of colonization and consolidation. The Spanish colonies were divided, initially, into two viceroyalties and a number of *audiencias* or colonial high courts subordinate to them. The viceroyalty of Mexico or New Spain was created in 1535 with Mexico City as its capital, and the viceroyalty of Peru or New Castile, created in 1542, had its capital at Lima. Over the five centuries during which Spanish colonial government evolved, new viceroyalties and *audiencias* were created, and changes occurred in jurisdiction, status and location.[1]

There were three major forces in the early days of the Spanish colonies, which often conflicted with one another. There was first the secular state, run by an expanding bureaucracy which claimed control over all persons in the colonies; secondly there was the Catholic Church which was anxious to convert the Indians, prevent their exploitation and create a Christian society; and thirdly there was the *encomendero*, or upper class, consisting of former *conquistadores*, and other Spaniards.[2] Although they were not the only seekers for land and wealth, it was among this third group that the most adventurous entrepreneurs could be found. Irving Leonard has written vividly about them:

> The New World offered an outlet for the tireless energy of leaders long habituated to war, and for the restless ambition of disinherited second sons . . . who were prone to resist the absolutist tendencies of the crown . . . [Thus] many military expeditions, subsidized for the most part by their commanders, poured out of Spain and, from . . . Santo Domingo and Cuba . . . overran with their few thousands the vast reaches of two continents in almost as few decades . . . [seeking] large dividends and quick returns. Gold they wanted . . . [and] landed estates . . . with peasant serfs . . . Such holdings the feudal lords might enjoy . . . and then pass

. . . on to their heirs . . . This lordly grandeur was . . .
most prized, and feudal fiefs in the New World had the
advantage of remoteness from the restraints of an increasingly absolute monarchy . . .[3]

The new lands were colonized through the *encomienda*,
the granting by the Crown of the use of Indian land and
labor. The recipients of the *encomienda*, called *encomenderos*,
were given the right to extract tribute from the Indians. Although the Crown recognized the value of these privileges
in attracting settlers to the new colonies, it was at the same
time hesitant to allow the development of a powerful aristocracy which could create conditions like those in Spain
before the accession of Ferdinand and Isabella. Consequently, a struggle ensued between the *encomenderos* and
the government that was to continue throughout the sixteenth and seventeenth centuries. The Crown wished to
facilitate the mining of precious metals which could be sent
back to Spain; but in their turn the colonists demanded the
right not only to collect tribute from the Indians, but to
keep a percentage of the ore's value. The Crown refused to
grant the *encomenderos* inheritance in perpetuity, but inevitably over the course of time the most valuable land slid into
the hands of wealthy Spanish and creole families, some of
whom were the descendants of *conquistadores*.

The Church recognized the need of the colonists to
employ Indian labor in mines and farms, but they condemned any efforts, often violent, to enslave Indians. The
Crown also frowned upon violence. In 1542 Indian slavery
was officially abolished, although Indians continued to
work under conditions which were not far removed from
slavery. In Mexico and Peru, which had highly developed
civilizations at the time of the initial conquest by Spain, mil-
lions of Indians perished from the effects of forced labor
and from European diseases — smallpox, typhus, measles,
influenza and others — to which they had no immunity.[4]
Partly because of the resultant drop in Indian population,

African slave labor was introduced into colonial plantations in the tropical coastal areas. The Crown and the Church voiced no objections to slavery of Africans; the Church itself used African slave labor, which, by the end of the sixteenth century, was widespread in Latin America.[5]

Shortly after the conquest, offspring of mixed Spanish and Indian parentage (*mestizos*) began to appear in the colonies, as a result of both rape and willing cohabitation.[6] It was customary for *caciques* or local chiefs to bestow women as gifts upon the conquerors as evidence of good will. Indian women were available to the Spanish, as domestics and as laborers on the estates and in the mines. In the upper classes of Aztec and Inca society, *mestizos* were accepted freely, although these societies were as rigidly stratified as Spanish society. *Mestizos* became leaders in the Indian communities, serving as intermediaries with the conquerors. Certainly for Indian women marriage to Spaniards often meant better lives than their own people could offer them.[7] Within fifty years of the conquest, both Crown and Church were becoming concerned about the number of *mestizos* in the colonies, which had been envisioned as a replica of Spain in America. Although sexual relations outside marriage were of course strongly discouraged, the Spanish were not rigidly opposed to intermarriage between Indians and whites as they were to any sort of fraternization between whites and Africans. Nevertheless, sporadic attempts were made to discourage Spanish-Indian marriage: land policies, for instance, were instituted to confine Indians and Spaniards to separate communities. But the authorities had to recognize that, apart from the fact that the two groups were economically dependent upon each other, there were simply not enough Spanish women in the colonies to provide marriage partners for the colonists.

Since early population records are unreliable, it is impossible to determine the number of colonial Spanish women, but it has been established that only a few women accompanied the *conquistadores*. Colonial records do show that in Mexico and Peru, the centers of Spanish colonial civilization in the sixteenth century, Spanish women began to arrive within ten years after the cessation of the violence and insecurity of the initial exploration and conquests. By 1550 women appear to have constituted about ten percent of the Spanish population. Until the seventeenth century, in areas settled later, like the Río de la Plata in southern South America, women probably constituted no more than five to twenty percent of the Spanish population. The few Spanish women who came to the small settlement of Buenos Aires during the sixteenth century either died along with their men of starvation, disease or at the hands of hostile Indians, or gave up and went home in discouragement. It was not uncommon, until the seventeenth century, for Spanish men in Buenos Aires to request and receive permission to marry their Indian concubines although on occasion colonial officials would demand that an *encomendero* who was living with an Indian woman send to Spain for his wife.

Government policy encouraged men to send for their wives and other female relatives; land grants, at one point, were restricted to men with Spanish wives. Strong pressure was not needed; everyone recognized that Spanish women were needed as a stabilizing and civilizing force, and that the loose sexual environment of the early colonial period had to end. Most settlers were seeking status; some, who belonged to the *hidalgo* class, Spain's secondary nobility, had come to America because Spain was overrun with aristocrats and its resources were running out. For people who wanted to climb socially, noble titles were available for sale in the new world, as they were in old Spain. Adventurers could rise to the aristocracy through advantageous marriages with women of the nobility; then they could accumulate land and establish themselves as respectable landed aristocrats. Spanish wives were necessities if these dreams of status were to come true.

What little is known about Spanish colonial women is more or less limited to those of the upper class, since the cultural and religious life of the colonies centered around them. Kinship has always played a dominant part in Latin American society; nepotism and the use of political office for personal advantage were already common in the colonial period and, as members of important families, women participated in the complex web of kinship systems that evolved over the years. Although the law appeared to exclude women from any influence at all, it has been noted recently that women were not powerless in the colonies. Since the family was the basis of business and community life, married women had more de facto power than the Spanish legal system seemed to allow them. It is recognized now that aristocratic women managed large agricultural haciendas, bought and freed slaves, established entails and founded convents and charitable institutions and, in fact, were important and influential in various aspects of colonial life and in the alliances that transmitted power and money from one family to another.

On the surface at least, the social and legal position of colonial women was determined by traditional Spanish institutions, according to which women were the property of the males of the family. Spanish law, from which colonial law derived, was based on Roman law, which codified the supremacy of the husband and father. In addition the Moorish occupation of Spain, from 711 to 1492, had imposed the Islamic custom of the seclusion of women which, although never as overpowering in Spain as in Moslem countries, was nevertheless a social factor. It did not in practice extend to women of the lower classes because of economic necessity and because lower class families lacked stability. In Spanish America the practical problems of a frontier society militated against the adoption of seclusion of upper-class women, although it remained an ideal and status symbol for some families, especially those who came from Southern Spain where centuries of Islamic domination had had a powerful impact.[8]

The confusing and often contradictory inheritance laws of the kingdom of Castile were transferred to the colonies. Although primogeniture existed, it was not the general rule. The laws of inheritance dictated that all property acquired during a marriage belonged equally to both partners, and that at the death of either spouse the survivor was entitled to half the estate, the other half then being divided equally among all children of the marriage, male and female alike. The survivor's portion, in its turn, was treated in the same way. The exception was the *mayorazgo* or entailed estate.[9] It is not known how often the *mayorazgo* excluded women. Inheritance laws were complicated further by the colonial system of land distribution. As a rule, women were excluded from ownership of *encomiendas* and other land grants. Asunción Lavrin has said that *encomiendas* were given to women only as a form of royal patronage for the wives and daughters of the early *conquistadores* and settlers and did not indicate sexual equality.[10]

Under the Spanish civil code, women, along with children and the insane, were legally classed as imbeciles. Married women existed entirely under male authority; single women remained *patria potestad* or under the rule of their fathers until they were twenty-five years old, after which they gained some civil rights and could marry without their fathers' approval; at that time they lost their rights again, although they could, with their husbands' written permission, initiate legal action in connection with their own income or property which they had acquired before marriage. Some prominent families tried to protect their daughters by demanding that husbands agree to allow their wives some independence after marriage. Married women did customarily control the income from their dowries, the amount as a rule being a minor part of the couple's total income. Widows were prevented by law from acting as heads of estates; because of this and other pressures, widows sought to remarry as soon as they decently could in order to avoid confiscation of their property. In a few instances widows had sufficient power and prestige to supervise their property, although even these were under societal pressure to remarry. And they were closely watched by authorities for evidence of mismanagement of their estates. A male relative sometimes claimed that an estate was being mismanaged by a widow or by an unmarried woman over twenty-five years old; the courts would uphold his right of kinship to protect his family's patrimony, and appoint him guardian of the estate. Thus more or less throughout their lives, women remained subject to their families. One need hardly add that women were expressly forbidden to hold political or administrative positions in the colonies. The ideal woman, the saying went, left her home only three times: to be baptized, to be married and to be buried.[11]

Under these circumstances, it is not surprising that many women welcomed convent life in the profoundly religious colonies. From 1540 to 1811 fifty-seven convents were founded in Latin America; by 1800 there were twenty-two in Mexico City alone. Much of the wealth which accrued to the Church from the reconquest of Spain and the conquest of the New World was invested in the building of convents — along with, of course, monasteries and churches. Colonial convents, often heavily endowed, offered women freedom from patriarchal constraint and an opportunity for educational development; they relieved society of the responsibility for unmarried respectable women and gave these women a rich community life.[12] In an era when most women were illiterate, and only a few upper class women received even a rudimentary education at home, there were educated nuns.[13]

One of these was the Mexican Sor Juana Inés de la Cruz (1651-1695), who was for several years the poet laureate of the Mexican viceregal court. She had been a child prodigy, writing lyric poetry when she was three and learning Latin at eight, after taking only twenty formal lessons. When she was twelve she asked her parents to allow her to attend university disguised as a boy; however, although she was much admired at the viceregal court, no one there would sponsor her for the university. With that door closed to her she decided when she was fifteen to seek her education as a nun, and entered the Convent of the Discalced (or Barefoot) Carmelites, a strict order that had a library of over twelve thousand volumes. However after two difficult years she left the Carmelites, where she found life too harsh, and entered the convent of San Jerónimo in the center of Mexico City. There, while she worked with the poor, she studied, in addition to Christian doctrine, such secular subjects as linguistics, pedagogy and science. For a few years her intellectual accomplishments won her praise, but in the late 1680s her criticism of colonial social inequities and her interest in scientific observation brought her into conflict with local representatives of the Inquisition which discouraged intellectual curiosity and frowned on any departure from Christian revelation as the means of knowledge. Sor Juana had criticized the insensitivity of the Church to the needs, spiritual as well as material, of the poor, and the hypocrisy and lax morality of the colonial upper class. The result was a threat of excommunication. After months of mounting pressure from the powerful Bishop of Puebla, Don Manuel Fernández de Santa Cruz, and from her own lifelong friend, the Portuguese Jesuit Antonio de Vieyra, the harrassed nun succumbed and abandoned her intellectual pursuits. After that she declined both mentally and physically, gave herself over to excessive acts of penance, including self-flagellation, and died at the age of forty-three, a martyr to the cause of intellectual freedom.[14]

Today Sor Juana is something of a heroine to feminists. It is remembered that she wrote of her need for privacy in order to work, a need that was anathema to a society that demanded the total dedication of women to the needs of the family, Church and society. Her poetry has been preserved, including romantic poetry that demonstrates her sympathy with the plight of women, and her recognition and rejection of the double standard for sexual behavior. She criticized society's attitude toward prostitutes:

> Ignorant men who accuse
> Women wrongly,
> Without seeing that you cause
> The very thing that you condemn.
>
> If with unequalled fervor
> You solicit their disdain,
> Why do you expect them to be virtuous
> When you encourage them to sin?
>
> You combat their resistance
> And then, gravely,
> You say it was their weakness
> That accomplished your end.
>
> Whose is the greater guilt
> In a sinful passion,
> She who falls to his lure
> Or he who, fallen, lures her?
>
> Or which is more rightly to be reproached,
> Although both are guilty,
> She who sins for pay,
> Or he who pays to sin?[15]

The persecution of Sor Juana must be viewed in the light of Spanish culture of the time. After its golden age in the early sixteenth century, Spain turned its back upon the Renaissance and gave itself up to the narrow, harsh and sterile spirit of the Inquisition, the excesses of which outraged even the Papacy and which remained a Spanish institution until its long overdue abolition in 1820. Anyone could be accused by the Holy Office, not just Jews, Protestants and erring intellectuals, but even Church and secular officials and important colonials. There was no appeal from the decisions of the Inquisition's tribunals; the threat to life and property was real and the power of the Inquisition extended to every facet of colonial life. The Counter-Reformation sought to shelter the colonies from religious schisms and from European cultural trends in general. In 1543 the Crown prohibited the exportation to America of most works of fiction and ordered the censorship of most books on secular or religious matters deemed delicate. Seventeenth century Spanish scholasticism was medieval and totally rejected European work in science and philosophy. These attitudes had a deadening effect upon Spain, preventing economic and political development.

By 1700 Spain had lost economic control of its American empire.[16] The Latin American mining boom lasted only from 1545 to 1610; more than two-thirds of the silver from the mines of Mexico and Peru went to pay Spain's debts and did not circulate in the Spanish economy. During the seventeenth century a decline in silver production was added to the effects of an inefficient and corrupt colonial administration and an aristocracy, both peninsular and colonial, devoted to conspicuous consumption instead of capitalist investment. Since Spain had never developed a commercial bourgeoisie, it had no textile, iron or paper industries; thus both the mother country and the colonies were forced to import goods from Holland and France. By the 1690s Spain controlled only five percent of the trade with its colonial possessions, even though it had a legal monopoly of trade. A third of the local trade was in Dutch and Flemish hands, a quarter belonged to the French, one-fifth to the Genoese, one-tenth to the English and a small percentage to the Germans. Metals from colonial mines stimulated the general economy of Europe, but not of Spain. As Eduardo Galeano said, "Latin America was a European business."[17] In addition to all this, political disunity was rife, stemming in part from the inability of the Crown to weld Spain into a modern nation and in part from a series of dynastic crises.

Thus by the end of the seventeenth century Spain was in drastic decline; it could not pay its debts. Rival European powers were encroaching upon the colonies, physically as well as economically, and the creole upper class was chafing under Spanish rule. It was obvious that the Spanish colonial system could not survive without a drastic overhaul.

With the death in 1700 of Charles II, the last Hapsburg monarch of Spain, the throne was taken by the French Bourbons, under whom Spanish America experienced what has been called "a new imperialism." The Spanish Bourbon Kings [Philip V (1700-1746); Ferdinand VI (1746-1759); Charles III (1759-1788); Charles IV (1788-1808)] desired to protect French economic interests against the English in both Spain and its colonies and to increase the control of the monarchy over the creole elites. They instituted a series of reforms of colonial administration and of defense and attempted to revive colonial commerce, encouraging the colonies to import goods from Spain — a somewhat futile enterprise because of Spain's lack of industry. Through complex restructuring, colonial administration was made more efficient, while the structure of society was preserved. The Spanish Bourbons were not revolutionaries, but reformers. The new corps of colonial administrators were told that they must serve the Spanish state rather than their own region. The Bourbons intended that they should help to curb the economic and political power of the colonial Church and the creole aristocrats, which was increasing at the expense of the Crown.

The Bourbons succeeded: the general quality of colonial leadership improved as a result of their actions. Their economic and political reform brought the colonies closer to the mainstream of European progress and ultimately increased the confidence of the creole upper class in their ability to rule themselves. In that way the Spanish Bourbons might be said to have planted in the colonies the seeds of the destruction of Spanish imperialism. During the Counter

Reformation and the Baroque Age the Spanish Crown had encouraged xenophobia and suspicion in its people. However with the reign of the Bourbon King Charles III, the previously closed and hostile Spanish state was opened to French intellectual and artistic influences; interest arose in rationalism and experimental science, and literature, art and architecture flowered. This political, intellectual and artistic liberalization profoundly and permanently affected Spanish America, where there was a consequent emphasis upon public works and civic responsibility, and where the upper classes welcomed this fresh spirit of inquiry and open-mindedness. The cultural horizons, especially of lawyers, writers, artists and government administrators, widened, and they began to travel to Europe and to bring back previously proscribed French, Dutch and English books: novels, scientific tracts, political philosophy and other kinds of social criticism. They fell in love with European culture and were eager to be part of everything modern and progressive. Inevitably, Spanish culture began to appear to them to be backward and unenlightened.

Although the Spanish Bourbons did not set out specifically to improve the status of women, their progressivism did open participation in civic life and cultural endeavors to women. There was also the new interest in secular education, which came to the colonies from France. The French *philosophes*, translations of whose works were popular in the colonies by the 1760s, were engaged in lively discussions of the value of women's education to society and to the women themselves as social beings. Rousseau and Voltaire took the position that women should serve society by continuing to serve men. Condorcet and d'Holbach, on the other hand, believed that women should be educated to play a political part in their communities.[18] The discussion was not confined to France. In 1739 Benito Feijoó, a Spanish priest, wrote *The Defense of the Vindication of Women*, in which he said that women were not intellectually inferior to men and that they should be educated. The opposite view was taken by Fernández de Lizardi, a Mexican, who argued that females were morally superior to men and should spend their energies on the moral improvement of their families and contribute in that way to the betterment of society. In 1745 the Count of Campomanes, an influential advisor to Charles III, held that women should not be idle, but should contribute their labor to society: upper class women were morally corrupted by idleness, a tradition more common in southern Spain than in the rest of the Iberian peninsula or in the colonies. In 1790 Doña Josefa Amar y Borbón, an upper class Spanish woman, wrote a pamphlet arguing for liberal education of women including moral and physical training to prevent them from wasting their lives in pursuit of personal beauty and the attentions of men. Society, she said, should recognize women's potential and their contributions to the family by helping them to lead interesting lives and fulfill themselves.[19] Whether these tracts were widely read is not so important as the fact that they were appearing in Latin America for the first time.

Throughout the eighteenth century there was a growing tendency for upper class women to involve themselves in cultural activities. For instance, branches of the Societies of Friends of the Country, an organization started in Spain in 1785 to support the arts, were founded in several colonial cities. All over Spanish America women organized to patronize the arts, especially, as we have noted, the arts of France. Charles III allowed women to be admitted for the first time to the *Sociedad Económica* of Madrid, an unprecedented step, and in 1783 decreed the founding in Madrid of several free schools for girls. He urged that other Spanish and colonial cities follow this example. The creoles did not respond; female public education was almost non-existent in the colonies until after the wars for independence. However the lives of some colonial women were changed by increased secularization, urbanization and industrialization and the general intellectual expansiveness of the eighteenth century Enlightenment; although women were barred from the universities, education for women was considered a viable subject for discussion and women of the upper classes were allowed to help in the creation of a new cultural environment. This was especially true in Mexico City, Lima and Buenos Aires.

The Bourbon enlightenment found fertile soil in Buenos Aires, which lay in an area that had been a backwater of Latin America and was both underpopulated and underdeveloped. Since it had been settled later than other colonies, the area of the Río de la Plata was less closely allied to Spain; colonials were accustomed to more economic freedom in that area than were their counterparts in Mexico and Peru. Charles III and Charles IV wished to consolidate hitherto unexploited portions of the colonial empire in order to protect that empire from the increasing encroachments of other countries. This policy was a response to the approaches of England and Portugal to the southwestern portion of the continent; the policy was most evident in the southern cone of South America.[20] In 1776 the viceroyalty of the Río de la Plata was created, to centralize fiscal and administrative control over what is now Argentina, Paraguay, Uruguay and part of Bolivia. It spanned the continent from Tierra del Fuego in the south to Upper Peru in the north, and from the Atlantic in the east to the Andes in the west. It was from this viceroyalty that Argentina developed as an independent country in the first decades of the nineteenth century.

In 1536 the first Spanish expedition arrived in what is now the province of Buenos Aires. They were in search primarily of gold and silver, planned on instant riches and had brought their women with them to help build a prosperous, stable colony. They christened the first large river they came upon the Río de la Plata, or River of Silver. However they soon discovered that the pampas, the grasslands of southeastern South America, contained no precious metals: the silver owned by the indigenous people had been obtained through trade with the silver-rich Indians of Peru. This grave shock was followed by the discovery that the Indians of the pampas, the Quarandí, were hostile, and would neither work nor provide food for the colonists who had therefore to give up their plans and return to Spain or settle in the north, in Asunción, Paraguay, where the Jesuits were helping to build a colony and where the native population, the Guaraní, were co-operative.

In 1556 Isabel Guevara, the wife of Pedro Esquivel, a leader of the abortive Río de la Plata colony, wrote to the Crown to bolster a petition she and her husband had made for a grant of land in Paraguay and the use of Indian labor there; she described in detail the tragic events of 1536: the disease and starvation which the Spanish endured and their violent confrontations with the Quarandí, as well as the zealous loyalty with which the would-be colonists had embarked upon their mission. Whether the family's petition was granted is not known, but Isabel Guevara's letter is a memorable document, which makes clear that the conquest of the Río de la Plata was the most difficult of the Spanish conquests of the New World. Unlike the Incas of Peru and the Aztecs of Mexico, the Indians of the pampas had no structured civilization which could complement the civilization of the Spaniards. These Indians were hunters who plundered the settlements and carried off the settlers. Spanish women were warned against attempting to settle in the region of the Río de la Plata.

However, after several failed attempts, intrepid colonists were finally able to establish the post of Buenos Aires in the estuary of the Río de la Plata in 1580. The conquered Indians, relatively few in number, were distributed among the settlers as laborers under the system of *repartamiento*, a system of forced labor. Beginning in 1590 Portuguese slavers brought Africans to Buenos Aires; most of them were sent on to plantations in northern Argentina and Upper Peru, or Chile. In the port city slaves worked mostly as domestics, a fact which led inevitably to miscegenation. By the late 1770s there were several thousand Africans and mulattoes in Buenos Aires, half of them free, who became silver workers, hat makers and did other artisan work.[21] As whites continued to emigrate from Spain, they quickly overran available positions in government and commerce and they too became artisans.

A hundred years or so were to pass before the Spanish awoke from their preoccupation with the search for precious metals to realize that the rich black soil of the Argentine was a treasure in itself, one of the world's most fertile areas. Consequently Buenos Aires remained for a long time a largely neglected port city, while the cities of the Argentine interior — Córdoba, Salta, la Rioja, Catamarca, Jujuy, Tucumán — grew rapidly because they were important bases for the Peruvian mines; Córdoba especially became a religious and intellectual center during the seventeenth and eighteenth centuries. That these cities could be reached overland from Chile and Bolivia was another reason for the neglect of Buenos Aires, which was too unstable and unprofitable to attract settlers. It was an open city, without police, where bandits, pirates and smugglers came and went freely.

By 1650 the conquerors' dream of discovering the gold-filled cities of the Caesars and the Indian paradise of Trapalanda had dissolved, and interest was growing in the area's natural resources, and in trade.[22] The port of Buenos Aires began to be used for the export of hides and sugar to Spain from the interior. However, the policies of the Crown interfered drastically with the city's development, because before 1776 Buenos Aires was under the jurisdiction of the viceroyalty of Peru and merchants could not legally export to Spain from the Argentine port, but only to Lima. John Gunther has called it fatuous

> . . . that Buenos Aires, on an estuary leading im-
> mediately to the Atlantic, and facing Spain across the
> ocean without any . . . obstacles, was forced to conduct
> all its trade via Lima, the viceregal capital of Peru, so
> that Lima would derive the exclusive benefit; this
> meant that goods had to be shipped by mule across the
> Andes to Lima, all the way from the Atlantic to the
> Pacific and in the precisely wrong direction, then up
> the Pacific coast by sea to Panama, then across the isth-
> mus by land, then by sea once more to Spain. It was as
> if — today — Chicago had to trade with New York via
> San Francisco and Alaska.[23]

In 1776, this situation was remedied, although difficulties continued to crop up: with the creation of the viceroyalty of La Plata trading policies were reformed, and
Buenos Aires became a legal military and commercial shipping center. The city began to grow; by the eighteenth
century it was preoccupied with commerce. In 1750 the
population was twenty-five thousand; in 1780 fifty thousand and in 1810 four hundred thousand in approximately
one million square miles. Of these, fifty-three percent lived
in the Andean provinces and forty-seven percent in the littoral provinces.[24] The landowners expanded their estates;
their cattle waxed fat on the rich grasslands. In addition to
food, of which jerked beef was to become an important export, cattle supplied hides, half of which were exported to
Holland.

Argentine society was racially hierarchical: whites constituted about thirty-eight percent of the population. In addition to Spanish immigrants and creoles, many Portuguese
had arrived from 1580 through the seventeenth century to
make Buenos Aires an important link in a chain of Portuguese coastal trade cities. They remained despite persecution and some attempts at expulsion. These whites
owned the choicest city properties, the first lucrative trading permits and the rights to herds of wild horses and cattle.
They ranked above *castas*, people of mixed race, and blacks,

who by 1810 constituted about thirty-two percent of the population. The remainder of the population were Indians, who by that time lived outside Spanish jurisdiction. Both Indians and blacks worked the land, while *mestizos* joined the militia, worked on cattle ranches or ran artisan shops.[25] Throughout the eighteenth century the region of the Río de la Plata grew, while Spain, ironically, declined in power and wealth. Creoles seized the opportunity to fill the economic and political vacuums which occurred because of Spain's futile involvement in eighteenth and early nineteenth century European dynastic disputes. From 1793 to 1795 Spain fought alongside Britain and her allies against the armies of revolutionary France. These wars were disastrous for Spain, ending in defeat and an enforced alliance with France which pitted Spain against England from 1796 to 1808. This alliance with Napoleon led to the British invasion of Buenos Aires in June of 1806, an invasion unplanned and unauthorized by the British government.

The Spanish viceroy, the Marquis of Sobremonte, fled in a panic to Córdoba. For two months the city submitted to the presence of British forces under Sir Home Popham, while London delighted in the prospect of trade with South America; Napoleon had cut off England's European markets. A second expedition was hastily put together, to be accompanied by seventy ships filled with trade goods. Suddenly, while these preparations were going on overseas, Buenos Aires exploded into rebellion: the British force was defeated and Popham was stranded on his ships in the estuary. The second English expedition arrived, led by General George Whitelocke, and took Montevideo but was forced into retreat by fierce resistance in Buenos Aires from both the militia and the people. That ended British attempts to take the port city.[26]

This victory greatly increased the self-esteem of the *porteños*, as the people of Buenos Aires were called, and increased also their contempt for the Spanish monarchy

because of the flight of the viceroy and the easy defeat of
the regular army. *Porteños* had been left to their own devices
by Spain and they could see that they could handle their
own affairs. They had their own heroes: Martín de Alzaga,
a lowly born Basque and successful businessman, and Santiago Liniers, a French born soldier in the regular army who
had formed the militia of separate regiments of creoles,
blacks and Spaniards, most of them of humble origin, who
had driven out the British. In 1807 Liniers became interim
viceroy; he refused the Crown's request to disband his
army, and he and Alzaga took over the government of
Buenos Aires. In September, 1807, Napoleon invaded
Portugal and in March, 1808, Charles IV, the Spanish King,
was forced to abdicate in favor of Joseph Bonaparte, Napoleon's brother. A revolution ensued in Spain in the interests
of Charles' heir, Ferdinand VII, imprisoned by the French.
Britain now became Spain's ally.

In Buenos Aires there was a power struggle between Alzaga and Liniers, resulting at least in part from the lifting by
Liniers in 1808 of restrictions on the importation of British
goods, an act which brought in enough increased revenue
to allow the payment of salaries to the militia, made up
of about thirty percent of the male population. This
strengthened Liniers' position. In August, 1809, Viscount
Balthasar de Cisneros arrived from Spain, took control of
the city from Liniers, and revoked Liniers' liberal trade policy, upsetting the economy and causing talk of rebellion.
When in May, 1810, news came of the fall of Seville to the
French, the *porteños* took the step which had been threatening since Cisneros appeared. An assembly of colonial
citizens (*cabildo abierto*) quickly passed motions naming
themselves the legal controllers of the city, since the fall of
the Spanish government had led to the collapse of the viceregal administration in Buenos Aires. On 25 May Cisneros
was officially deposed and arrested by Cornelio de
Saavedra, head of the militia and a central figure in the

coup. The new government junta then took office, with Saavedra as president. Among the members of the junta were Mariano Moreno, Manuel Belgrano and Juan José Castelli, all strong free traders.

Although the new junta wished to extend its power over the rest of the viceroyalty, where there was much dissatisfaction with Spain, all the territories would not accept this. Loyalists took control in Montevideo and Asunción and swore allegiance to the Spanish Council of the Regency, which had replaced the junta of Seville. Liniers was a central loyalist figure in Córdoba, where he sought to revive his career by supporting Spain; thus in upper Peru and Córdoba loyalist armies were quickly marshalled. The result was an abortive war, victory for the *porteños*, and death for the loyalist leaders.

A split occurred in the junta itself: Mariano Moreno wanted a declaration of independence, proclamation of a republic and the centralization of power in Buenos Aires; Saavedra wanted self-rule, with the appearance of allegiance to Spain and a loose confederation of territories with shared power. In 1810 Moreno attempted a coup; when it failed, he chose exile and died en route to Europe. Saavedra duly enrolled delegates from the territories in the junta, which was called the *junta grande*, and established local *juntas provinciales* in the hinterlands. Nevertheless, fighting persisted in Upper Peru and in Paraguay between loyalists and the armies of Buenos Aires; the result was the establishment of the independent republic of Paraguay in 1811 and the creation of Bolivia in 1825. Juan José Castelli, representing the junta in Upper Peru, infuriated the creole elites by attempting to abolish allotments of Indian labor and in Paraguay Manuel Belgrano endured military defeat.

The situation had evolved so that the territories sought independence not only from Spain but from Buenos Aires as well. Their movement came to be called Federalist, its goal being a loose confederation of independent provinces.

Opposing this was Buenos Aires Unitarism. A triumvirate succeeded Saavedra, dissolved first the *junta grande* and then the *juntas provinciales* and took a hard line toward the territories. The secretary of the triumvirate was Bernardino Rivadavia, a creole intellectual allied with Manuel Belgrano, whose ideas for strengthening the local economy had had a republican tinge when he had first formulated them in the 1790s. But the new Unitarists preferred monarchy to republicanism: they made overtures to England because they wanted British support, although they did not want to be taken into the British orbit. The Federalists of the interior, wanting republican self-rule, hated free trade because it lowered the employment rate of their artisans and hurt their markets. The first triumvirate fell in October, 1812, and was succeeded by a second triumvirate which lasted until January, 1814.

The second triumvirate, in favor of emancipation from Spain, organized a congress, being careful to include fair representation from the interior. The congress declared itself in control of what was now called the United Provinces of the River Plate, and enacted a number of reform measures, reminiscent of the actions of the French Assembly in 1789: Indian labor allotments and tribute and the *encomienda* (which in any case had fallen into disuse) were abolished, along with the Inquisition and judicial torture. Inherited titles were annulled, the slave trade was outlawed, although slavery was not, but the children of slaves were freed, as were slaves who entered the Provinces from abroad. Most of the cities and territories of the interior were renamed as provinces with their own autonomous governors. At the same time the second triumvirate adopted a free trade policy which played havoc with the regional economies, and was forced to raise troops and money for the expensive war against Spain. Thus tension continued between the Federalists, powerful in the provinces, and the Unitarists who were increasingly popular in Buenos Aires.

The result of emancipation from Spain was civil war, which was to plague the misnamed United Provinces of the Río de la Plata for seventy years. As an example of the chaos which ensued, it can be noted that the province of Buenos Aires in 1820 had twenty-four governors, leadership changing every two weeks. The wealthy descendants of military men and government officials were in constant conflict with one another over local and national issues, to say nothing of personal ones. In the provinces regional warlords, *caudillos*, grew in power and independent republics were declared. *Caudillos* fought not only against Buenos Aires but often against one another in a series of small civil wars. The Unitarists, led by men like Rivadavia, wanted continuity between the Bourbon reign and new self-rule. They came to emphasize the importance of Buenos Aires, while the Federalists fought centralization in the capital and in the two powerful provincial cities. Two of their greatest grievances were taxes and forced service in the military. The *caudillos*, former militiamen, put together armies made up of peasants, slaves and vagrants, called *gauchos*, basically setting the countryside against the cities. In 1819 two *caudillos*, Estanislao López of Santa Fe and Francisco Ramírez of Entre Ríos, invaded Buenos Aires in protest against the policies of Juan Martín de Pueyrredón, who had been elected director of the Congress in 1816. They were victorious and were able to dictate terms to the *porteños*; central authority had disintegrated.

The presence of British merchants grew in Buenos Aires after 1810; they were able to overcome both Spanish and native business competition and by 1813 had flooded the market with goods from Lancashire and the Midlands and taken over shipping and the hide trade along with, importantly, the purveyance of munitions. Local businessmen, squeezed out, began to concentrate increasingly on cattle ranching, and cattle products, including meat-salting, became important exports throughout the Americas.

In 1821 the alliance collapsed between the *caudillos* López and Ramírez; Ramírez was killed and López too weakened to continue to threaten Buenos Aires. Rivadavia re-entered public life and became a government minister. By the following year the Provinces were ready to discuss a national constitution. Rivadavia was by and large a liberal: he helped to write and pass a new extension of the suffrage and he supported free trade, foreign investment in the country and the cultivation of land by European immigrants. He fought a winning battle against the clergy on the question of tax exemptions and tithes, reformed the administration of the port city and established the University of Buenos Aires, with state funding. In addition he established the Beneficent Society, a secular women's charity organization, also funded by the state. In 1826, when Rivadavia was named president of the United Provinces, he formulated the Law of Emphyteusis under which the state granted long-term rights of access and use to lands remaining state property. The subsequent rental fees were to be used to reduce duties on imported goods and the onus of payment was to be put on the cattle ranchers and plantation owners rather than on the *porteño* merchants.

The plan was a failure. Available land was quickly taken, and ranching profited rather than trade. Since the lessees were allowed to set the evaluations on the land, the inevitable consequence was under-evaluation. As if this were not bad enough, the government had no mechanism to collect the rents. Land speculators gobbled up land merely by registering claims and there was no limit to the amount of land any lessee could claim. Thus acres of land accumulated in a few hands and cattle ranches grew with no visible benefit to the *porteño* merchants. During the 1820s twenty-one million acres of public land were transferred to the control of five hundred people.[27]

Rivadavia favored close ties with Britain in the hope that foreign capital would encourage local business and banking. By 1822 almost all of Buenos Aires' imported manufactured goods were British, and by 1824 there were thirteen hundred English living in the city, most of them in the export-import trade. In response to the numerous economic concessions granted them, the British in 1824 officially recognized the United Provinces and the two countries signed a Treaty of Friendship, Navigation and Commerce, granting each other favored status in trade, along with freedom of religion, exemption from military service and security of property for residents.

In 1826 Rivadavia's administration produced a constitution which declared a republic, with a president, a congress and separation of powers on the United States model. The provinces were given self-government and a share in the revenues of Buenos Aires. These arrangements were intended to please the Federalists; what did not please them was a presidential term of nine years and the right of the president to appoint and dismiss provincial governors. In addition, provincial militias would be disbanded, provincial levy of taxes abolished and provincial debts cancelled in return for cession of land to the national government so that land could be offered to lessees under the Law of Emphyteusis. Finally, Buenos Aires would be detached from its province and made the seat of government.

This constitution was rejected by the *caudillos* who did not trust Buenos Aires sufficiently to rely on it for revenue or disband their own militias, and they disliked Rivadavia's reformist attitude to the clergy. In the city, Rivadavia's special treatment of the British angered the cattle interests, who were also suspicious of the plan to separate the city from its province. When war broke out between Brazil and the United Provinces, Rivadavia seized the opportunity to defeat the Brazilians and then turn his army onto the provinces and force their compliance with the proposed constitution. But he did not foresee the expense of the war, nor that a blockade of Buenos Aires would cause exports to plummet, nor that the government's printing of paper money would lead to an inflation. Both the British merchants and the cattlemen turned against the president; when four provinces banded together in a military alliance against the government, Rivadavia was forced to resign. Once again there was civil war.

Rivadavia's successor, Manuel Dorrego, attempted to pacify the *caudillos* by dropping the government's insistence on ratification of the constitution and any suggestion that the provinces should be subject to the rule of the port city. The name of the United Provinces was changed to the Confederation of the River Plate. Dorrego made peace with Brazil, but the return of the armies caused more disruption: Dorrego was taken prisoner and shot by soldiers under General Juan Lavalle, who attempted to take Buenos Aires for the Unitarists, but was himself deposed by General Manuel de Rosas (1793-1877). In 1829 Rosas became governor of Buenos Aires, ending two years of anarchy.

Although he was a Federalist, Rosas was given dictatorial powers by the legislature of Buenos Aires; ironically, power in the provinces was held by a Unitarist, José María Paz. Rosas remained in power, with a brief hiatus between 1832 and 1835, until 1852. He inherited anarchy, with rampant inflation and a depression caused by war and drought. He formed an army and used censorship, exile and general intimidation to keep his critics quiet. His own interests lay with the ranchers, but he was admired by the urban poor, even though he cut spending in the city and increased it threefold in the provinces. During a civil war in the interior Rosas was able to destroy the power of Paz; the *caudillos* then called for a Federalist constitution which would give them both autonomy and a share of the national revenue. Rosas put them off while he consolidated his power, using the Church, the Army and a personal police force to bring a terrorized peace to the country. He propagandized fiercely for Federalism, intimidating, exiling and murdering his enemies. He neglected the courts, the *junta de representantes*, the University of Buenos Aires and British investment, preferring open trade with other countries. Many prominent *porteño* families were forced to flee, either voluntarily or through formal banishment. Montevideo in Uruguay was a gathering place for these exiles; many others went to Europe and the United States.

By the 1840's the economy had improved; exports doubled between 1837 and 1852. Rosas abandoned Emphyteusis and granted land according to military rank; soldiers then sold their land to the ranchers, who thus increased their holdings. Rosas encouraged private ownership by those who had leased the land under Emphyteusis. He raised protective tariffs because he did not wish to burden landowners with taxes. These policies especially hurt French merchants in Montevideo, who joined their complaints to those of the French residents of Buenos Aires. Rosas was hostile to foreign culture and especially to French culture, which he rightly identified with sophisticated Unitarist attitudes inimical to his own brand of rural traditional Catholicism. The result of this friction was a French blockade of Buenos Aires in 1838.

In order to overcome the economic difficulties caused by the blockade and the ensuing invasions and civil wars, Rosas had to maintain a large standing army, and find the revenue for it. He besieged Montevideo in order to bring more trade to Buenos Aires, and he tried to prevent provincial trade with England and France by controlling the traffic on the Paraná River, which led to another blockade of Buenos Aires, this time by both the French and the English; once more he used the military to overcome his enemies. In 1848 he closed the Paraná since no one had the power to prevent him. However he incurred the enmity not only of many South American countries but of his own provinces, particularly the province of Entre Ríos which had large cattle and sheep ranches and which was firmly under the control of the *caudillo* Justo José de Urquiza, a landowner determined on trade with other provinces and other countries. Unfortunately for Rosas, Urquiza had his own military and eventually, when he could not convince Rosas to open the Paraná, he mutinied, with support from Brazil and Uruguay. In late 1851 he marched on Buenos Aires, where Rosas' popularity was at a low ebb because of abuses perpetrated by his large army and because of his stinginess toward his own bureaucracy. By early 1852 Rosas had been defeated. His life was saved by the British who took him to England on a British ship, since despite his hostility toward Europeans Rosas had built a huge export business with the English. Many of Rosas' followers remained behind to be massacred by Urquiza's troops.

As might be expected, Rosas left a stagnant country, which, except for emancipation from Spain, remained much as it had been forty years earlier. The Unitarist movement was, however, alive in Montevideo where so many of its supporters had fled. Most influential was a group of Unitarist intellectuals called the Generation of 1837, who accepted European ideas. They believed in authoritarian government and put emphasis on material progress. The three most famous members of the Generation were Esteban Echeverría, Domingo F. Sarmiento and Juan Bautista Alberdi. Echeverría had been forced to flee Buenos Aires in 1838, accused of pro-French activity because he held literary salons and disseminated emancipated ideas. Sarmiento, who had campaigned hard for popular education, had written a book attacking the Federalists and the *caudillos*. Alberdi was a follower of Alexis de Tocqueville and a believer in European immigration and colonization. This group of men worked tirelessly to prepare the Argentines for the period of liberal thought which they were convinced was at hand.

Despite the civil wars which followed on the heels of Rosas' defeat, the province of Buenos Aires ratified the

Constitution of 1853, establishing an elected two-house legislature, an independent judiciary and a bill of rights, and outlawing the slave trade, which was already in any case extinct. Restraints on trade were banned. To protect interior landed interests, a national Senate was set up, elections to which were put in the hands of provincial legislatures, and an income level was instituted for politicians. Suffrage was held to be a privilege rather than a right. The province of Buenos Aires had experimented with universal male suffrage in 1820; widespread corruption had caused the experiment to fail. The Constitution further declared Catholicism the state religion, although freedom of choice was established. The president's term was set at six years, and although he could not be elected to successive terms, he was given wide powers. Foreigners were exempted from forced loans and from military conscription. Each of the provinces, including Buenos Aires, was allowed its own militia.

This constitution was not ratified by the country until 1862 when an electoral college of provincial delegates chose Bartolomé Mitre to be the first president of what was now called the Argentine Republic. Mitre was a military man who had helped to defend Montevideo against Rosas and had been instrumental in causing the capitulation of Urquiza, who had maintained an army in the interior that was a threat to the central government in Buenos Aires. In 1860 Mitre had been named governor of Buenos Aires. On becoming president, he immediately set about reforming the country's institutions; in 1862 he set up a national treasury and customs office; in 1863 a national judiciary and national voting laws, and in 1864 a new national army. His popularity was enhanced by a boom in the sale of wool and a dispensation by him of revenue to the provinces. The British were lured back by the country's prosperity, so foreign funds were once more available for investment; under Mitre income was up, from exports and government spending. A war with Paraguay which lasted from 1865 to 1870 helped Mitre to reinforce his power with provincial cattlemen, because the troops used quantities of meat and leather. In the interior the situation remained chaotic, with regional governments changing frequently.

In 1868 Mitre was defeated by Domingo Sarmiento, who reaped the benefit of many of Mitre's undertakings: by 1870 a railway line was completed between Rosario and Córdoba, bringing the country closer together; in the early 1870s the country had the rudiments of a national postal system, a civil law code and two establishment newspapers, *La Prensa* and Mitre's organ *La Nación*. Federalism was by then generally discredited. The last *caudillo* of importance was Ricardo López Jordan, who took control of Entre Ríos after engineering the assassination of Urquiza in 1870 and who was himself deposed in 1874. The *caudillos* were gradually transformed from regional warlords to political bosses in the pay of the great landowners. Elections were a sham, serving only the interests of merchants and landlords.

Sarmiento was the first of four presidents who came from provinces other than Buenos Aires and who were supported by the National Autonomist Party (PAN). His particular interest was popular education; the new constitution provided that primary education was to be funded by the provincial governments and secondary education, including normal schools, by the national government. However because of a chronic shortage of money, lack of interest and corruption in the provinces and pressure from the Church, the national government was forced to support primary education in the provinces. Other reforms were prevented by the rivalry between Buenos Aires and the other provinces.

In 1880, under Julio A. Roca, the PAN candidate, the city was detached from the province of Buenos Aires and made capital of the republic. Provincial militias were disbanded and the province of Buenos Aires was forbidden to issue paper money. Argentina became at last a united nation. The new capital of the province of Buenos Aires was the city of La Plata, thirty miles from the old capital.

Despite these steps toward stability and pacification, inflation continued, along with unequal distribution of land, which actually intensified. In 1889 a group which was to be called the Civic Union began to agitate for political reform, particularly popular democracy. This agitation climaxed in a rebellion against the government of Miguel Juárez Celman, a somewhat autocratic Cordoban who had involved the country heavily with foreign investors. The Church supported the rebellion because Juárez Celman had legalized civil marriage and other measures seen as anti-clerical. Basically the rebels wanted economic changes to help their own interests. The rebellion was defeated, although it caused Juárez Celman to step down. Thus even though the country had been centralized and stabilized, the landed interests kept their grip on all attempts at land reform and, along with mercantile interests, on political power. This power was not to be successfully challenged until 1916.

In the late eighteenth and early nineteenth centuries, Argentine societal attitudes loosened, because of the influence of foreign culture, and French culture in particular. By the 1780s there was a large British contingent in Buenos Aires as well as colonial administrators appointed by the Bourbons, all of whom admired French ideas, considering them modern and progressive. Because of this, Spanish customs and attitudes began to appear backward and out-of-date. Some families began to make frequent pilgrimages to Paris; gradually a knowledge of French became a necessity for social, political and economic intercourse. It became fashionable to hire tutors to teach children French, and to speak French at cultural gatherings, which were organized mainly by women, who in this way began to emerge from seclusion. They founded cultural societies modeled on the French salons and men and women mixed freely at parties called *tertulias*, where books and philosophies were discussed and poetry reading and musicales were held. Women were responsible for the pleasant, elegant ambience of the salons, and often provided the musical entertainment. They gave tea parties at which they listened to readings from the works of Madame de Staël and Madame de La Fayette or to poetry modelled after the newest French verse.[28] Women also worked to raise money for charitable and cultural causes: in 1789, for instance, a group of *porteño* women organized a party to obtain funds for the construction of a printing works next to the municipal orphan asylum, to provide training and employment for the orphans. The women volunteered to supervise the printing works and to continue to raise funds for its maintainance.[29]

One influential woman was Rafaela Vera y Pintado del Pino (1753-1810) who in 1788 was appointed cultural advisor to the viceroy, Don José de Vertíz. Rafaela del Pino came from an enlightened family with a belief in the value of public education, a relatively rare attitude among the Argentine upper class, who held, on the whole, that there was no practical reason for mass literacy, although they thought that the Church should provide vocational training. Rafaela del Pino was an early proponent of public primary education and worked to improve the cultural climate of Buenos Aires, as well as for its independence from Spain. One of her daughters, Juana, was married to Bernardino Rivadavia, the politician.[30]

Another memorable woman was Joaquina Izquierdo (d. 1824), a patron of the arts who helped in 1817 to found the National Theatre. Since she did not marry, she had a measure of social freedom and financial independence. She was herself a poet, and held much admired readings of her own work and of French poetry.[31]

After 1806 the salon of María Sánchez de Thompson de Mendeville (1786-1868) was popular. Mariquita Sánchez, as she was affectionately called, was for three generations a leading figure in diplomatic and literary circles.[32] When she was fifteen her parents had chosen a husband for her; she rejected him because she was in love with her cousin, Martín Thompson, whom her parents considered emotionally unstable. In an unheard-of act of defiance Mariquita Sánchez went to the viceroy Sobremonte and asked his permission to marry her cousin. For some reason Sobremonte ignored the parents' wishes and complied with the girl's request and in 1805 the couple married. The union produced five children before, in 1817, Thompson unfortunately fulfilled the prophecies of his in-laws and went mad and died. In 1820 Mariquita married Washington de Mendeville, a Frenchman, whose behavior was so unattractive that the Sánchez family was forced to bring about his banishment from the colony.[33]

Despite this domestic upheaval, Mariquita Sánchez wrote poetry and essays, worked for independence from Spain and held a salon for artists, writers, diplomats, politicians and businessmen. During the reign of the dictator Rosas, she was a social leader of the exile colony in Montevideo where she carried on an active campaign against Rosas, which included ridicule of his daughter Manuela (1817-1898), who acted as hostess for the widowed dictator, giving balls and *tertulias*. The elegant ladies in exile made merry over Manuelita's provincial awkwardness and lack of education. But María Sánchez herself felt the lack of a formal education. In one of her poems she commented on the lives led by upper class women:

> The only things we understand
> are hearing mass, reciting prayer,
> arranging our ensembles
> and patching and repair[34]

In the 1820s María Sánchez, who believed that women should serve society in a productive way, became a prominent philanthropist, and she continued to write and to support the arts throughout her life.

Like Rafaela del Pino, Joaquina Izquierdo and María Sánchez, there were twenty or thirty culturally active women in Buenos Aires who came from important *porteño* families. There were Mercedes Escalada, Juana María Pueyrredón de Sáenz Valiente — these, among others, held and attended salons and were present at discussions of the major philosphical and political questions of the day.

In 1810 the Patriotic Literary and Economic Society of the Río de la Plata was founded under the auspices of the colonial government. Women were allowed to raise funds for its social events, although they were permitted only auxiliary membership in the Society, one stated pupose of which was to assist in the cultural and intellectual development of the colony's women. This kind of society was springing up throughout Latin America at that time; apparently the founders were not disturbed by the irony that women were customarily barred from full membership of organizations intended to help their social advancement, and lively discussions were held at meetings about the status of women in society. This was discussed also in the popular press. *Telégrafo Mercantile*, the first Buenos Aires daily newspaper, founded in 1801 by the colonial government, published, along with economic and political news, essays on education, health, philanthropy and general domestic issues. Men wrote on women's issues, transmitting the idea that upper class women as the core of the family, had a special, if vague, responsibility to society. A few writers advocated widening both women's privileges and responsibilities.

One of these was the political leader Manuel Belgrano (1770-1820) who published an article, originally written in 1797, holding that women needed to do more than imitate French customs; they needed to acquire skills that would give them some measure of economic independence and help them to become responsible citizens. He said that enlightened men should help women in practical ways by seeing that they received more social and intellectual freedom. On the whole the essays in *Telégrafo Mercantile* supported secular education for women and criticized the Church for maintaining that female education must be basically religious. It was believed that women remained superstitious and ignorant because what little education they received came from the Church; this religious education was thought by enlightened men to be responsible for women's weak sensibilities and supposedly hysterical natures. Religious education, they thought, encouraged irrationality, and secular education had to be the way to make women emotionally stable so that they could be better mothers and fit companions for intellectual men.[35]

Anti-clericalism was common among a wide range of the upper and middle classes in Buenos Aires at the turn of the nineteenth century. Freemasonry, introduced from Europe in the 1780s by French and British intellectuals, was highly critical of the temporal power of the Church, although it was not necessarily anti-religious. Both Manuel Belgrano and José de San Martín (1778-1850), Argentina's national heroes, were Masons; they were politically anticlerical, advocating the separation of church and state and consequent limitations on church power and privilege. But both were at the same time devout Catholics.[36]

The Bourbons, wishing in general to build the power of the state at the expense of the Church and of private business, held that education should be the responsibility of the state. In 1767 they expelled the Jesuits from Spanish America because the first loyalty of that religious order was to Rome and because it had become too wealthy and powerful. As a further measure, ecclesiastical revenues were confiscated by the state. The Bourbons sought to attack the Church through a viceroyalty of the Río de la Plata, but the influence of the Church was strongest in the provinces, which were more closely related than the port city to traditional Spanish institutions. The Bourbons did not intend to alter drastically colonial attitudes and customs; they felt that the Bourbon economic, political and social reforms would help gradually to develop a more sophisticated, progressive and secularized society. Nevertheless the interior of the country, where the Church remained firmly entrenched, remained conservative, religious and patriarchal in attitudes toward women.

The Church's role in the education of the poor had not been questioned. Convent schools provided vocational training and literacy for orphan girls, because it was believed that ignorance and lack of skills led women to a life of prostitution. The convent schools were a source of trained servants for the orphanages themselves and for the homes of the elite. The Bourbons helped to expand educational facilities in Buenos Aires convents, and to open new schools for girls. In 1801 the Colegio de Niñas Huérfanas was founded, primarily to train orphans to become nuns, although all the pupils did not take the veil. Sewing, knitting and embroidery were taught, along with ironing and hairdressing — skills for good ladies' maids. Another school, the Colegio de San Martín de la Ciudad de los Reyes, offered scholarships to young women who wanted to teach primary school. The students of both these schools came from the lower classes, but a few upper-class girls were allowed by their families to attend for want of a better alternative.[37] In one small private school where girls were admitted from the age of eight, the directress, Doña Josefa de Carballo, emphasized what she called "training for decency". The curriculum consisted of music, embroidery and physical education, the latter to prevent physical and emotional illnesses in females who led idle lives with little or no exercise. Literacy was a requirement for admission, which means that some girls learned to read and write before they were eight years old.[38]

Male intellectuals wanted girls not only to be literate, but to be educated to behave in a proper, virtuous and rational way so that they could emerge from the darkness of Spanish colonialism into the bright air of the Enlightenment and be entrusted with the education of their children which, among the upper classes, was customarily left to tutors hired by the children's fathers.

By the latter half of the eighteenth century, it was becoming apparent that traditional Catholic charity could not meet the needs of the masses. The urban poor increased greatly in population after Buenos Aires was made capital of the viceroyalty. Expanded social services were needed to alleviate the precarious economic circumstances of tradesmen and laborers. The Spanish Bourbons followed the example of the French and English governments and attempted to assuage urban unrest by instituting a system of poor relief which rested on financial co-operation between Church and state. Together they built hospitals, foundling homes and workhouses where indigent people could be housed and make some contribution to society.[39] Since at this time progressive thinkers were concerned with the question of useful occupations for upper class women, the increase in philanthropic activity was a welcome answer. Philanthropic work seemed to be the natural outlet for women's energies. They had been brought up to believe that they were obliged to help their social inferiors; thus their maternal feelings of concern for the sick and the underprivileged, coupled with their domestic talents and the amount of free time they had, was seen as a great potential asset for the government.

It was not new for women to help the sick. Throughout the colonial period laywomen's associations had customarily provided financial support for nursing given the poor by monks and nuns. Wealthy women contributed food and linens for this purpose. In the Bourbon era, however, women began to be involved directly in the day-to-day operations of new hospitals. In the 1760s upper class matrons were encouraged to work daily in several hospitals built in Buenos

Aires by the Spanish Bethlamite fathers with the support of the Crown.[40] And in 1789 women joined the Brotherhood of Holy Charity in maintaining a new women's hospital in the city. But as the women's involvement increased, they were not entrusted with decision-making positions; nuns continued to be the only women allowed to undertake any administrative responsibilities, and then only when there were no priests to take them on.[41]

This trend toward women's participation in state-supported charity continued throughout the nineteenth and into the twentieth centuries. It was during the Bourbon period that the idea took hold that such participation was not only a religious obligation, as it had traditionally been, but a civic responsibility as well. Several prominent women — María Sánchez de Mendeville among them — who held literary salons, also worked in philanthropic enterprises, encouraged by progressive upper class men.

During the British invasions of Buenos Aires in 1806 and 1807, and afterward during the period of early independence, women were involved; the British invasions seem to have awakened a deep national consciousness in *porteño* women.[42] Special female brigades were formed to provide nursing care and food for the militia and a few women were involved, accidentally, in combat. One of these, Martina Céspedes, was made a sergeant major by Santiago Liniers in 1807 in recognition of her bravery in the struggle against the British. In 1810 Tomasa de la Quintana and a group of women turned their salon into the Patriotic Society, which raised funds for the military; the women donated their jewels to the cause. During this period many women took on the management of family estates and businesses, in order to free the men to serve the country in one capacity or another. These women did not — courageous, independent and strong-willed as many of them were — have any idea of gaining political advantage through their activities for themselves or for women in

general.[43] Their involvement in the independence movement was regarded by everyone as temporary, a response to
unusual circumstances, and was applauded as such.
Numerous laudatory biographies have been published in
Argentina over the past eighty years, praising the selfless-
ness and bravery of modest *porteñas* who faded gladly into
obscurity after the achievement of independence.[44] It has
been suggested that women withdrew from political activities after independence because they never learned to
think politically or to regard themselves as political beings.[45] In any case societal pressure obviously required that
they slip back into normal female roles.

Although throughout the nineteenth century some progressive male politicians and intellectuals supported the expansion of women's public activities, the Constitution of
1853 itself did not improve the status of women. It offered
democratic principles, on the lines of the United States
Constitution, with religious liberty and citizenship for all
people born in the territories. However it had always been
in fact a sort of ideal on paper, having been suspended in-
numerable times over the years to satisfy the desires of
political groups or military dictators. And it is in parts
ambiguous. Article 21, for instance, states that all citizens
are required to take up arms when necessary.[46] Since
women were not allowed to join the armed forces, the court
ruled that Argentine women were not entitled to the
privileges of citizenship, including suffrage. Occasionally
women of property were allowed to vote in local elections,
at the discretion of provincial and municipal governments.
During the latter half of the nineteenth century several immigrant women were refused citizenship. One who received it was Julieta Lanteri de Renshaw; in 1911 she was
granted citizenship as a favor to her husband. It did not
bring suffrage with it and she was refused the right to regis-
ter to vote.[47] The matter of women's voting rights was
clarified in 1912 by the passage of the Sáenz Peña Law

establishing universal male suffrage; this law specifically denied women the right to vote in national elections.

Nineteenth century Argentine civil law was on the whole more restrictive to women than Spanish colonial law had been,[48] although nineteenth century civil codes were in the main a continuation of Spanish law, which denied women identities separate from their husbands.[49] During the nineteenth century Latin America civil law was based on the Code Napoleon. In 1870 Argentine civil law was codified in the Vélez Sarsfield *Código Civil* which contained the principles behind Argentine attitudes toward the family and property. Women were classed with unborn children, minors and the retarded and insane. Husbands were legal representatives of their wives; married women could not enter into legal contracts without their husbands' permission. Divorce was forbidden and legal separation, which freed the wife from the husband's legal supervision, could be granted to a woman only if she could prove her husband was insane. In these cases the mother was allowed to keep her children until they reached the age of five; after that, if the husband could prove himself capable, the children were given to him. Regardless of social status, mothers of illegitimate children and the children themselves had no legal rights and fathers were not obligated in any way to their illegitimate offspring.

Because of the sharp increase in population in Argentina after the middle of the nineteenth century, civil courts were overloaded and insufficiently funded; cases involving male abuses of family power were put aside. Both rich and poor women received short shrift, although in cases of "grave injury" the courts might rule in behalf of upper class women; the "level of culture" of the litigants was taken into consideration.[50] In general, however, domestic disputes, especially over money, were expected to be kept in the family. If there were financial neglect it was thought that women with wealthy families would seek help from their relatives, and women without such recourse would manage somehow.

An organized campaign for the granting of civil rights to women began in Argentina much later than in Europe and North America, probably because of the lack of an educated middle class, the influence of the Church and the almost constant political and civil turmoil which existed in the country during the nineteenth century. In fact, Argentina was ahead of other Latin American countries in beginning to work for women's rights: Buenos Aires was the most culturally advanced city in Latin America; Argentine women were better educated than other Latin American women and they involved themselves earlier in organized philanthropies. European immigration was another factor in the emergence of women from the shadows of family life.

Between 1859 and 1932 over five million people came to live in Argentina, mostly from Spain and Italy. Of these, ninety percent settled in the coastal provinces and of these ninety, sixty-five percent settled in the city of Buenos Aires. Argentina had 1-2 million native inhabitants in 1859. Between 1860 and 1914 immigrants caused the population to grow by sixty percent. In the 1860s forty-five percent of the population of Buenos Aires was foreign-born; by 1890 this had increased to ninety percent.[51] This massive immigration along with economic development helped to create a large and independent middle class as well as an urban proletariat.

Among the immigrants were liberal and Socialist political exiles, some of whom were educated professionals, whose presence in the country helped to break down the rigid Argentine class system, and to promote secular education and create a social climate in which a woman's movement was possible. The Argentine woman's movement began toward the end of the nineteenth century, following the lead of similar movements in the United States and Europe in which women began for the first time to organize themselves to work for the improvement of the lives of women and children and, ultimately, for the betterment of society. This woman's movement is not the same as the feminist movement, which can be loosely defined as the movement for female social and political equality.[52] Feminists frequently joined women's philanthropic, educational and temperance organizations, although the philanthropists and temperance workers did not necessarily join the feminists in their political demands. Many influential clubwomen in both Argentina and the United States were strongly opposed to feminism.

In Argentina feminism was largely an immigrant movement, and one closely allied to the Socialist party, although, as we shall see, there were some non-Socialist feminists. Argentine feminists like Alicia Moreau de Justo differed from North American feminists like Susan B. Anthony in that they subordinated women's issues to socialist issues. There were in fact few people in Argentina working actively and consistently for women's rights until after the first World War. It was not until 1926, when women in England and North America had won their suffrage battles, and the climate of opinion had caused even the Church to support reform, that Argentine women finally received their civil rights. And it was not until 1947 that they were granted suffrage — ironically — against the strongly expressed wishes of the Socialist feminists.

Notes

Abbreviations: *Hispanic American Historical Review (HAHR); Latin American Research Review (LARR); American Historical Review (AHR).*

[1] See Charles Gibson, *Spain in America* (NY: Harper & Row, 1966) and Barbara and Stanley Stein, *The Colonial Heritage of Latin America* (NY: OUP, 1970) p. 14.

[2] Gibson, p. 49.

[3] Irving A. Leonard, Introduction to Bernal Díaz del Castillo, *The Discovery and Conquest of Mexico, 1517-1521* (NY: Farrar, Straus, 1956), p. xii.

[4] Magnus Mörner, *Race Mixture in the History of Latin America* (Boston: Little, Brown, 1967), p. 31; Stein, pp. 37-38.

[5] Mörner, p. 112.

[6] Mörner, pp. 22-23.

[7] Elinor Burkett, "Indian Women and White Society: The Case of Sixteenth Century Peru," in *Latin American Women: Historical Perspectives,* ed. Asunción Lavrin (Westport, Ct: Greenwood Press, 1978), pp. 101-128.

[8] James Lockhart, *Spanish Peru, 1532-1560: A Colonial Society* (Madison: Univ of Wisc Press, 1968), pp. 150-170.

[9] Charles Boxer, *Women in Iberian Expansion Overseas, 1415-1815* (NY: OUP, 1975), pp. 52-53.

[10] Asunción Lavrin, "In Search of the Colonial Woman," in *Latin American Women,* p. 39.

[11] Lavrin, p. 30.

[12] Thomas Gage, "Mexico City, 1635" in *Impressions of Latin America,* ed. Frank McShane (NY: Morrow, 1963), pp. 26-39.

[13] See Susan Soeiro, "The Social and Economic Role of the Convent in Colonial Bahia, 1670-1800" in *HAHR* 54, no. 2 (1974), 209-232; Asunción Lavrin, "Women in Convents: Their Economic and Social Role in Colonial Mexico," in *Liberating Women's History: Theoretical and Critical Essays,* ed. Berenice Carroll (Urbana: Univ of Ill Press, 1976), pp. 249-271; Edith Couturier, "Women in a Noble Family: The Mexican Counts of Regla, 1750-1839" in *Latin American Women,* pp. 129-149.

[14] James D. Henderson and Linda Roddy Henderson, *Ten Notable Women of Latin America* (Chgo: Nelson Hall, 1978), p. 79.

[15] Henderson, p. 91.

[16] Eduardo Galeano, *Open Veins of Latin America,* trans. Cedric Belfrage (NY: Monthly Review Press, 1973), p. 37.

[17]Galeano, p. 35.

[18]Ann Pescatello, *Power and Pawn: The Female in Iberian Families, Societies and Culture* (Westport, Ct: Greenwood Press, 1978), p. 161.

[19]*Ibid*, p. 61.

[20]John Lynch, *The Spanish-American Revolution, 1808-1826* (NY: Norton, 1973), pp. 1-51.

[21]George Reid Andrews, *The Afro Argentines of Buenos Aires, 1800-1900* (Madison: Univ of Wis Press, 1970), pp. 23-41.

[22]R. B. Cunninghame Grahame, *The Conquest of the River Plate* (NY: Greenwood Press, 1968), pp. 281-284.

[23]John Gunther, *Inside South America* (NY: Harper & Row, 1966), p. 115.

[24]James Scobie, *Argentina: A City and a Nation* (NY: OUP, 1971), p. 61.

[25]Andrews, pp. 23-41.

[26]Lynch, p. 41.

[27]Lynch, pp. 28-35.

[28]Lily Sosa de Newton, *Las Argentinas de ayer y hoy* (BA: Editorial L. V. Zanetti, 1967), p. 28.

[29]Sosa de Newton, *Las Argentinas*, p. 29.

[30]Lily Sosa de Newton, *Diccionario biográfico de mujeres Argentinas* (BA: Artes Gráficos Chiesino, 1972), p. 389.

[31]Sosa de Newton, *Diccionario*, p. 182.

[32]Helen Percas, "Women Poets of Argentina, 1800-1950," Diss. Columbia Univ., 1972, p. 3.

[33]Sosa de Newton, *Diccionario*, p. 331.

[34]Percas, p. 12.

[35]Johanna Mendelson, "The Feminine Press: The View of Women in the Colonial Journals of Spanish America, 1790" in *Latin American Women*, pp. 198-218.

[36]Esteban F. Rondanina, *Liberalismo, masonería y socialismo en la evolución nacional* (BA: Ediciones Libera, 1965), pp. 64-75.

[37]Robert King Hall, "The Secondary School in Argentina." Diss. Univ. of Chgo. 1936, pp. 19-20.

[38]Mendelson, p. 204.

[39]Cynthia Jeffress Little, "The Society of Beneficence in Buenos Aires, 1823-1900," Diss. Temple Univ., 1980, p. 17.

[40]Little, p. 28.

[41]Lavrin, p. 12.

[42]Sosa de Newton, *Las Argentinas*, p. 28.

[43]Evelyn Cherpak, "The Participation of Women in the Independence Movement in Gran Columbia, 1780-1830" in *Latin American Women*, p. 221.

[44]For example, see Elvira Reusmann de Batolla, *El Libro do oro de la mujer Americana* (BA: A. de Martino, 1910); Sosa de Newton, *Las Argentinas*.

[45]Lavrin, p. 11.

[46]*The Argentine Civil Code together with the Constitution and Law of Civil Registry*, trans. Frank L. Joannini (Boston: Boston Bk. Co., 1917), xxxvii.

[47]William B. Parker, *Argentines of Today* (BA: Hispanic Soc. of America, 1920), p. 41.

[48]Pescatello, p. 182.
[49]*Civil Code*, pp. 25-67.
[50]*Civil Code*, p. 38.
[51]Gino Germani, "Mass Immigration and Modernization in Argentina," in *Masses in Latin America*, ed. Irving Horowitz (NY: OUP, 1970), pp. 289-330.
[52]See Hilda Smith, "Feminism and the Methodology of Women's History," in *Liberating Women's History*, pp. 369-384.

2

Women and Philanthropy
in 19th Century Argentina

In eighteenth and nineteenth century Argentina, the *gente decente* — literally the "decent" people — were the *porteño* upper classes, whose ancestry was basically European, and the provincial oligarchy, which was European and mixed European/Indian. The mass of the population were called the *gente de pueblo* or common people. In 1820 Argentina had about five hundred upper class families; by 1870 the number had increased to eight hundred. The family conferred social status; ancestry was far more important in Argentina than wealth.[1]

Since upper class women generally married when they were fifteen to eighteen years old, they often had as many as ten or eleven children; if a suitable husband had not been found for a girl by the time she was twenty-five years old, she was considered unmarriageable. In these arranged marriages, rarely protested by the women, the groom was frequently fifteen to thirty years older than the bride. One who protested, as we have seen, was María Sánchez. Another, whose protest was more dramatic and tragic, was Camila O'Gorman (1828-1848), the daughter of Adolfo O'Gorman, a wealthy, powerful supporter of the dictator Rosas. Camila's mother was Joaquina Pinto de O'Gorman, a member of an aristocratic colonial family, and her paternal grandmother was Ana Périchon de O'Gorman who scandalized society during her marriage to Edmundo O'Gorman by carrying on a passionate love affair with Santiago

Liniers, the hero of the British invasion of 1806: her family exiled her to Brazil where, as a leader of salon society in Rio de Janeiro, she became embroiled in several clandestine love affairs.

On the death of her husband, Ana Périchon de O'Gorman returned to live in seclusion with her son's family in the province of Buenos Aires. She had a profound effect on her granddaughter Camila, who read romantic novels and sympathized with her father's enemies, the Unitarios. She found a sympathetic fellow-romantic in the local parish priest, Ladislao Gutiérrez, whose Federalist family was prominent in the province of Tucumán. Despite struggles against this illicit passion on the part of the priest, the couple ran off to the province of Corrientes where they taught school under false identities. In 1848 they were discovered and arrested by the Federalist army. Although Camila was pregnant, the couple were executed by order of President Rosas, Adolfo O'Gorman having refused to intercede on his daughter's behalf. This was an excessive punishment even by nineteenth century Argentine standards. Upper class women involved in illicit relationships were usually exiled or confined to convents; occasionally an erring priest was executed, but it was more common for them to be exiled or imprisoned. This young couple were the victims of the desire of Juan Manuel de Rosas to strengthen his ties with the Church and to demonstrate to the people that he was capable of acting against members of the upper class.[2]

Both María Sánchez de Mendeville and Camila O'Gorman have become romantic heroines to modern Argentine women. They are remembered because they rejected the cloistered stagnant life of the married woman. But little is known about those women who remained in the control of their husbands: their names did not usually appear in the family *sucesión*, the inventory of family possessions drawn up after the death of the male head of household. Although after Argentina declared independence from Spain the inheritance laws were revised so that half the estate was to go to the widow, and the other half divided among the legitimate children, these laws were often circumvented. The *sucesiónes* did not list all the property; because of the desire to avoid taxes and sometimes for other reasons property was hidden from the courts. Sometimes families formed corporations (*sociedades anónimas*) which transferred lands to chosen children; it was common for sons to inherit the greater part of the estates, while daughters, who were given the *quintas*, or summer houses, rarely inherited land of any significance.[3]

The range of activities was depressingly narrow for upper class women who could not, of course, work outside the home. For several decades, before the establishment in the 1870s of clubs from which women were excluded, salons provided women the intellectually stimulating opportunity to discuss the issues of the day with men. Bernardino Rivadavia did not believe that salons were enough to occupy women; he deplored their exclusion from civic life and believed that the vanity and superficiality for which upper class women were criticized was the fault of society which required of them only that they be domestically decorative. He wanted to include women in the building of the nation so that they could promote public morality. For these reasons, during his tenure as minister from 1821 to 1825 in the administration of Martín Rodríguez, Rivadavia founded the Beneficent Society, patterned after the French Philanthropic Society, a charitable organization run by women and supported by state funds. From the French Rivadavia took the idea of the establishment of shelters for needy women and annual awards of money to women who demonstrated moral strength in the face of great adversity. This Society, Rivadavia hoped, would ultimately enrich the lives of all Argentine women — the poor, who fell all too easily into prostitution, and the rich, whose idle lives affected their health.[4]

At the Society's opening ceremonies on 2 January, 1823, Rivadavia said:

> The social status of women is still too vague and uncertain ... This imperfection of civil society has placed many obstacles in the path of the progress of civilization ... It is eminently useful and just to give serious attention to the education of women, to the improvement of their customs and the means through which they achieve their basic necessities, so that we may pass laws which establish their rights and responsibilities and assure them the happiness which they deserve ... [5]

The Society was given the responsibility of founding schools and administering all state charitable facilities and educational institutions for women, including all state-supported Catholic charities and some schools for boys. The Society's members were appointed by the minister. During the first year, thirteen women were chosen; in ensuing years the number was expanded to twenty-five, at which it remained. The original thirteen members were given the responsibility of appointing new members to replace those who retired or died, a system which of course perpetuated the *porteño* elite administration of the Society, and also helped to determine its political cast. Twelve of the original thirteen came from Centralist families. Later in the century the Society's membership reflected the country's dominant political persuasions. There was an element of nepotism too: it was common for two or three members of the same family to serve the Society at the same time.

The majority of the women chosen were wives and mothers. There were two widows among the original thirteen — not surprisingly, in a society where girls were married at a young age to considerably older men. The Society provided a useful existence to these widows, whose children were grown. There were two childless wives among the thirteen.

María Sánchez de Mendeville was the first woman appointed by Rivadavia, to help him organize the Society's structure and choose the founding members. Among these were Cipriana Viana de Boneo (1777-1840), who had been educated by foreign tutors, was married to a naval officer and was particularly interested in vocational training for women; Estanislada Cossio de Gutiérrez (1791-1871) a cousin of the executed priest Ladislao Gutiérrez, who had spent her childhood in Paris, had married at fourteen a man of forty-two and was devoted to cultural pursuits; Justa Foguet de Sánchez (1787-1852), a cousin of María Sánchez de Mendeville, a salon frequenter and the country's first noted woman painter; Bernardina Chavarría de Viamonte (1782-1832), who was married to a military leader and Centralist politician and who founded and administered, during her tenure with the Society, the Catalina School for girls; and Mercedes Lasala de Riglos (1763-1837), who, as the oldest and most experienced charity worker of the thirteen, was appointed first president of the Society.

Four of the thirteen were single women. Since religious careers were not as popular for unmarried women in Argentina as they were in other more traditional Latin American countries, wealthy single women often administered households for their male relatives, who were frequently widowers with young children. The Beneficent Society offered interesting activities with social involvement.

Among the single women chosen for the initial group was Joaquina Izquierdo, the poet and heroine of the independence movement. She helped to plan curricula for the Society's primary and secondary schools, but unfortunately died a year after the society was formed. The youngest founding member was María Rosario de Azcuénaga (1801-1840), doubtless appointed to secure the support of her influential family. Isabel Casamayor de Luca (1788-1866), who suffered from a debilitating facial palsy, translated educational manuals from French and English and served several terms as inspector of the San Telmo School for girls. The most interesting of the single women was probably Josefa Gabriela Ramos Mejía (1766-1832), who, in 1812, had disguised herself as a man in order to join the army and fight for independence. After she was discovered and sent home, she donated all her money to the cause. Rivadavia chose her, among other reasons, because she had strong familial ties to the Church and he wished to quiet fears that he was anti-clerical. Señorita Ramos Mejía spent nine years working in the orphanage system and most of her lifetime attempting to recruit upper class women to charity work.[6]

Rivadavia was thought to be anti-clerical because of religious reforms carried out between 1820 and 1829; among them was the abolition of tithes and the codification of religious toleration. But religion was the foundation of the principles of the Beneficent Society, and the Church profited greatly from its support for their orphanages, hospitals and asylums which, in the main, had been underfunded and inefficiently run. The Church and the Society worked amicably together. Rivadavia did, however, limit the amount of money the Church could contribute to the Society because he wished the Church role in the administration of government-supported charity to be largely advisory.

The Society was funded by private donations as well as by the central and provincial governments. It was Rivadavia's plan that the nation's social assistance should come partly from the state and partly from the "maternal hearts of Argentine womanhood."[7] Fines for gambling were turned over to the Society and funds were raised in an annual government-supported Charity Day. But the Society's goals always outstripped its funding. These women saw poverty first-hand and became continual lobbyists for improved facilities and techniques. They were Argentina's first social workers, and the first women to be given important social and administrative responsibilities which had formerly been relegated to the Church. The Society founded and reorganized hospitals, asylums, orphanages and homes for wayward and indigent girls and women. In 1852 it took over the administation of the state hospital for women, the largest hospital in the country. In the course of the nineteenth century, the Society became the administrator of Argentina's entire welfare system, and it was responsible also for providing medical care during natural disasters and civil disorder.

From its inception the Society was charged with the establishment of a national primary school system for girls and with reorganizing and maintaining the *Colegio* of Buenos Aires, a primary, secondary and vocational residential girls' school, which had been founded in 1755 and run by the Brotherhood of Charity. The *Colegio's* small secondary school provided, under the Society, training for primary schoolteachers until 1878, when it became a vocational school for orphan girls. It must be remembered that until the beginning of the twentieth century most Argentines, and almost all Argentine women, were illiterate. The National Census of 1869, the country's first national census, reported that 25.2% of the male population was literate, as compared to 18.3% of the female population. In 1856 the government, aware of the need for improvement, had established a national department of education, and because of the work done through this department and the demands made by European immigrants, the census in 1895 showed an increase in literacy to 49.2% for men and 41.5% for women.[8] Until the 1870s all the primary and secondary schools for girls in Buenos Aires were administered by the Beneficent Society. The executive board appointed directors and staff, the majority of whom were women: widows and unmarried women with some education but no income. In this way the Society was able to provide employment for unfortunate friends and relatives of the executive board. As might be expected, during most of the nineteenth century workers in the social service system — including nurses and teachers — were inadequately trained.

This is not to say that the members of the Society ignored available information. On the contrary, they studied foreign social welfare policies and adapted those plans which seemed useful to them. One was the Malthusian workhouse theory, intended to encourage "the worthy poor" to better themselves. The Society wished to provide more than custodial care; they wished to imbue the objects of their charity with patriotism and religious morality. To this end they adopted also the Lancaster system of residential vocational training for poor children. Rivadavia had encountered this system on his travels in England, and he had suggested that the leaders of the Society study it and see if it could prove useful in Argentina. Primary schooling and vocational training in a relatively supportive atmosphere were the foundations of the system, which was used in workhouses and prisons for purposes of rehabilitation, although it was considered particularly valuable in orphanages where young children could be molded before they sank into a life of poverty and crime. It was instituted first at the Good Shepherd Asylum, which the Society ran with the Sisters of Charity.[9]

Both boys and girls in the schools run by the Society were trained for work, the boys in the building and printing trades and the girls as housekeepers and domestic servants. Girls did all the housekeeping in the orphanages and were taught to sew, knit, launder and iron. Many of them went to work in the households of the members of the Society and their families and friends.

Despite all these efforts, however, orphan girls often slipped into prostitution, the regulation of which was another of the Society's concerns. The president of the Society voted on the National Council of Hygiene, which had been created by the government to help contain the spread of venereal disease. Registration and regular physical examinations were mandatory for prostitutes; this was legislation supported by the Society.

As we have noted, no sizeable middle class existed in Argentina — or indeed anywhere in Latin America — to provide professional health and educational services until the late nineteenth century when there was an influx of educated European immigrants. It was not until 1886 that a professional nursing school opened in Buenos Aries, although girls were trained in the *Colegio* to work in the Women's Hospital. These were the only full-time health workers in Argentina. Even as late as the first decades of the twentieth century the ladies of the Society rejected any suggestion that women might be trained to be doctors.[10]

As in the case of nurses, primary school teachers in Buenos Aires, poorly trained as they were, came from the normal schools run by the Society. In 1876 the Common Education Law was passed, creating a General Council of Education. But the Society's main philanthropic institutions continued under their aegis until 1948 when these institutions were integrated into the Department of National Social Assistance by President Juan Perón, who wished to end the Society's control over social services partly for political reasons, to demonstrate his independence of the oligarchy, and partly for personal reasons because the Society had snubbed his wife. Perón also took steps to expunge the contributions of the Society from textbooks and histories.

The selfless woman was the Society's ideal — indeed, it was the Latin American ideal and possibly the world's ideal in the nineteenth century, at least. To that end each year during the formal ceremonies marking the anniversary of its founding, the Society awarded prizes, in the form of financial assistance, to those women who that year had exemplified the noble, moral core of the poverty-stricken family. The names and accomplishments of the recipients of these awards are listed in the Society's annual books of minutes (*Libro de Actas*). The women who won awards in the second decade of the twentieth century displayed the same admirable traits as those who had won in the third decade of the nineteenth century. In 1916 two working class heroines were honored:

> Filomena Tinanelli, widow, age 35
>
>> She had given birth to eighteen children of whom thirteen are living and all well educated. Her home is a model for all Argentines. She works as a seamstress during the day and takes in ironing at home during evening hours.
>
> Carmen de Ritis, age 26
>
>> She lost her father and supports her mother and various other relatives with her embroidery, by giving sewing lessons and, when this is not sufficient, she works as a servant. She needs money desperately because her mother needs an operation.[11]

In addition to giving some help to poor women, the Society provided paid employment for middle-class women as inspectors, nurses and teachers; the pay was poor, but it was pay nonetheless. The Society's accomplishments were impressive considering its limited personnel and information. It helped poor women to learn basic skills and trained some for teaching and administrative jobs in its institutions. The Argentine branch of the International Council of Women and other women's organizations of the late nineteenth and early twentieth centuries grew because of the experience Argentine women had had in the Beneficent Society, so indirectly from these philanthropic efforts and directly from the educational system, a woman's movement developed in Argentina.

Notes

[1] James Scobis, *Buenos Aries: Plaza to Suburb, 1870-1910* (NY:OUP, 1974), pp. 208-226. See also Diana Hernando, "Casa y Familia: Spatial Biographies in Nineteenth Century Buenos Aires," Diss. Univ. of Cal., 1973.

[2] Enrique Molina, *Una sombra donde sueña, Camila O'Gorman* (B.A.: Corregidor, 1984).

[3] Hernando, pp. 9-10.

[4] Little, pp. 42-67, 137-182.

[5] Decreto de creación de la Sociedad de Beneficencia, B.A.; 2 January, 1983. In the Archivo General de la Nación.

[6] Biographical information on the founding members of the Beneficent Society is found in Sosa de Newton, *Diccionario biográfico*, and in Hernando, p. 121.

[7] Decreto de creación, p. 16.

[8] Nancy Caro Hollander, "Women in the Political Economy of Argentina," Diss. Univ. of Cal., 1974, pp. 165-167.

[9] See *Actas de la Sociedad de Beneficencia, 1823-1946* (B.A.) in the Archivo General de la Nación. Also S. Madrid Páez, *Sociedad de Beneficencia de la Capital: Su misión y sus Obras* (B.A.: Talleres Gráficos de Huérfanos, 1923).

[10] Little, pp. 183-222.

[11] Sociedad de Beneficencia de la Capital, *Memoria de año 1916* (BA: Talleres del Asilo de Huérfanos, 1917), p. 43.

3

Education for Women
in 19th Century Argentina

"I firmly believe in the transmission of moral ap-
titude through organization. I believe in the infusion
of the spirit by means of speech and example."

Domingo Sarmiento[1]

During the 1830s and 40s, under the government of Juan
Manuel de Rosas, freedom in Argentina was sharply cur-
tailed. Rosas was a dictator who ruthlessly attacked those he
perceived to be his enemies. Although he had a close commercial relationship with England, his interest in British
institutions was limited to trade: he opposed the funding of
social programs, including public education, and the activities of the Beneficent Society. The core of his support lay
in the narrowly religious and conservative rural areas. His
own daughter, Manuela de Rosas de Ezcura (1817-1898),
was poorly educated and consequently socially inept. Although she attempted, on the death of her mother, to cope
with the social responsibilities connected with her father's
office, her performance was apparently never more than
adequate, and possibly less: she was ridiculed by women like
María Sánchez de Mendeville, who commented that Manuela, when well into her twenties, read and wrote like an
eight year old.[2]

Many prominent families fled Argentina because of
Rosas; many women active in the Beneficent Society could
not remain in Buenos Aires during his term in office. But

despite the culturally arid atmosphere of the time, some intellectual women stayed and worked in the capital. One of these was Petrona Rosende de Sierra, a salon hostess who, for a few months in 1830, published a twice-weekly literary magazine called *La Aljaba* (literally, *Tremor*), in which she advocated the adoption of European educational theories. Women, she said, must have faith in their own capacity for improvement before they could advance in society; they must prove their ability to overcome the resistance to female education of men and the Church. The government should provide primary and secondary education to females, teaching them not only basic literacy, but obedience, loyalty, and above all, to think rationally, so that they could fulfill their maternal role with dignity and without being distracted by frivolities.[3]

Another interesting woman was Rosa Guerra (d. 1868), the principal of a small private girls' school in Buenos Aires founded by Ana Bevins, a member of a prominent British immigrant family. In 1852 Rosa Guerra edited *La Camelia*, a magazine devoted to issues of interest to women, which she had persuaded Ana Bevins to fund. Unlike Petrona Rosende de Sierra twenty years earlier, Rosa Guerra believed that women did not need to prove themselves worthy of education, but had a moral and legal right to it; *La Camelia* protested the refusal of Argentine society to give them that education, which Rosa Guerra presented as a panacea; it would solve women's problems, give them self-respect and make them fit companions for educated men. At the same time *La Camelia* warned that women must not lose their feminine modesty; they must avoid giving an impression of intellectualism which could be equated with loose morality. The motto of *La Camelia* was "Liberty, not license. Equality between the sexes." During its brief life the magazine supported dress reform, a touchy issue of the time. Fashionable women's clothing was both expensive and uncomfortable; women, the editor said, dressed like ornamental dolls. Men might enjoy looking at them, but these fussy, fragile clothes did nothing to improve relations between the sexes. Despite her emphasis on the importance of modesty in dress and bearing, Rosa Guerra came under fire from influential Catholic women and from the Church. She was accused of attempting to alter the God-given role of wife and mother. Father Miguel Navarro Viola said, shortly after the first issue of *La Camelia* appeared, that women should not aspire to be journalists, nor, in fact, to be in the public eye in any way. And they should not be educated beyond basic literacy. Possibly because of this negative reaction, *La Camelia*, like *La Aljaba*, ceased publication after only a few months. However, two years later, in 1854, Rosa Guerra started another publication called *La Educación*, similar in format to *La Camelia* and dedicated to the "honorable ladies of the Beneficent Society and to all the fair sex of Argentina." Most of the articles, on literary, pedagogical and philosophical subjects, were translated from English and French. Those written by Argentines appeared under pen names: Rosa Guerra signed herself "Cecilia". The political slant of the journal was strongly Unitarist.[4]

Rosa Guerra was a prolific writer who, in addition to her magazines, produced novels, children's books and articles and poetry for the daily newspapers, both under her own name and as "Cecilia". In *Julia and Her Education*, probably her most important children's book, she described the difficulties encountered by a young girl in her struggle to get an education. Despite her liberal politics, Rosa Guerra believed that women were born to suffer because of their emotional dependence upon men, who could exist without love, while women could not. They could derive some satisfaction only from trying to help their sons and husbands understand the meaning of deep emotional commitment. In her work female self-sacrifice is a constant theme: women sacrifice themselves for lovers, for husbands, for children, for families, for the nation. This romantic conception of womanly martyrdom was a dominant theme in mid-nineteenth century Argentine women's literature. Women's patriotic poetry often extolled female virtues at the expense of men's selfishness. Self-sacrifice was the norm. "Just as the flower cannot live without air," Rosa Guerra wrote, "so the female cannot live without love."[5] A somewhat sentimental melancholy is characteristic particularly of her poetry, through which, indeed, often runs genuine despair:

> Oh sad heart! Why do you leave me in this state?
> Why are you always so restless and excited?
> Why do you breathe with such cruel sighs?
> Calling death with such eagerness.[6]

In February of 1852 Rosas was defeated at the battle of Caseros and fled to England. For the next nine years, until the government defeated the rebels at the battle of Pavón, Argentina was torn by civil wars. From 1862 to 1912, when universal suffrage was enacted, members of the Argentine Senate and electoral college were chosen by provincial legislatures. In their turn, the Senate and the college elected the President of the Republic. Like the provincial legislatures, the Chamber of Deputies, or lower house, was elected directly by male citizens who qualified for a franchise limited by literacy and property requirements.

After 1862 the government was occupied with immigration and the expansion of public education. Immigration, especially from northern European countries, was encouraged, as was intermarriage between immigrants and Argentines. As a result, by 1874 the annual number of immigrants had grown to 70,000 a year, as opposed to 6000 in 1862.[7] The liberal politicians who succeeded Rosas believed that public education, both primary and secondary, was the key to a stable society: they believed that educated masses would not fall victim to dictators who played upon their emotions. The government's educational programs were only moderately successful. By 1884 the number of children attending primary school in the province of Buenos Aires had increased over the 1852 figure by fifty percent. In the other provinces the percentages varied from fifteen to forty percent: in prosperous Entre Ríos forty to fifty percent of the children attended primary school, while in backward Tucumán province the figure was only fifteen percent. It can probably be said that the educational as well as the economic gap betwen urban and rural areas of Argentina widened during the nineteenth century, and that by the end of the century most of the rural provincial population remained illiterate.[8]

The Constitution of 1853 required that the provincial governments pay for primary education, and the federal government pay for secondary education, including normal schools. But because of the poverty and corruption in the provinces and the hostility of the Catholic Church to public education, (which it was feared would lead to greater secularization of society, especially in the light of heavy Protestant immigration), the national government was forced to assume a large portion of the financial burden for primary education in the provinces.[9]

It was Domingo F. Sarmiento (1811-1888) who helped to make Argentina a leader in education among Latin American nations. Sarmiento, who was Minister of National Education from 1854 to 1856, Governor of the province of San Juan from 1862 to 1864, Ambassador to the United States from 1865 to 1867, and Minister of Education for the province of Buenos Aires from 1874 until shortly before his death, considered his work in education to be the most important of his life.[10]

He was born in the Andean province of San Juan, descended from two distinguished families, the Sarmientos and the Albarracines, both of which had become impoverished at the beginning of the nineteenth century. Consequently Sarmiento received little formal schooling, although he was tutored in the classics by his uncle, Don

José de Oro, an erudite priest who had a strong positive effect on the young man's character. Sarmiento became involved early in women's education by teaching his younger sisters to read and write. In 1835 he became a teacher and in 1839 opened in San Juan the first provincial women's secular secondary educational institution. Sarmiento was imprisoned in his home province because he had refused to pay arbitrary fines imposed by the *caudillo* Juan "Facundo" Quiroga for imaginary or minor infractions of the law; these were actually forced contributions to the *caudillo*, who terrorized the province, slashing off heads, cutting throats and mutilating the bodies of his enemies. Consistently, Sarmiento was openly critical of the Rosas regime and was forced in 1842, in order to escape capture by the *mazorca*, Rosas' secret police, to flee to Chile, where he became a leader of the Argentine exile community, editing a newspaper called *The Argentine Herald*. In addition, he wrote several books on various topics, including politics, founded an educational journal and put together the first spelling textbook in Latin America. In 1843 he founded a normal school in Santiago for men and women, funded by the Chilean government; it was the first public teacher training institution in Spanish America. He served as principal of the school until 1847 when he was appointed Chilean Ambassador to Washington.

He travelled widely throughout the United States, studying educational systems in New England, the mid-Atlantic and Midwest. He was impressed not only with the constitutional freedom and educational and economic opportunites of the United States, but with the relative social, economic and educational freedom enjoyed by North American women. He visited for several months in West Newton, Massachusetts, with Horace Mann and his wife Mary, both prominent educators. In 1837 Horace Mann (1796-1859) had set up the Massachusetts primary and normal school systems, which he administered until 1848 when he entered the House of Representatives as an anti-slavery Whig. He served in the House until 1852, after which he became president of Antioch College in Yellow Springs, Ohio, a post he held until his death. Both Mann and Sarmiento considered education a panacea for all national problems, economic, social and political. Mann urged Sarmiento to work for the adoption of North American teaching systems in Argentina, simply translating the materials into Spanish. Good normal schools, he said, were essential if the primary schools were not to suffer. Costs would be cut considerably if women instead of men were employed as teachers; women were naturally patient with young children and were happy to be able to earn any money at all. As a bonus, employment as teachers would offer unmarried women a much-needed respectable and emotionally satisfying alternative to motherhood.[11] These comments Sarmiento found very much to his liking. His association with Dr. Mann was valuable to him; after the latter's death, Sarmiento kept up a voluminous correspondence with Mary Mann, who kept him informed about the latest pedagogical news.[12]

In 1851 Sarmiento returned to Argentina to join with General Urquiza to overthrow Rosas; in 1856 when Urquiza became president, he appointed Sarmiento Minister of Education. At last Sarmiento's hope of designing a first-rate educational system for Argentina could come to fruition. His primary desire was to close the great educational gap between the elites and the masses by separating the public school system from the Church, which he considered a reactionary relic of Argentina's barbaric past. In his most famous written work, *Life in the Argentine in the Days of the Tyrants; or Civilization and Barbarism*, a novel about the violent life of the *caudillo* "Facundo" Quiroga, which had started out as non-fiction, Sarmiento made the point that the supporters of Quiroga and Rosas represented Creolism, the Spanish American past, which lived on in the provinces and could be rooted out only through the growth of cities. Education was the instrument he intended to use on behalf of modernism and against traditionalism. A new generation of schoolteachers, mostly women, would begin the task.

In 1841 Sarmiento published a series of articles in the Chilean newspaper *Mercurio*, in which he cautioned girls against letting themselves be trapped into marriage by mothers and mothers-in-law. Education would provide them with an alternative to loveless arranged marriages. Educating women was in the national interest: motherhood was a grave responsibility for which education was necessary. Mother love was by no means sufficient. And Sarmiento believed that girls should be educated not only for motherhood, but with the ultimate goal of participation in public life and politics; he felt that local government was an extension of the home. After women had been educated and had had practical experience in local politics he thought, they should be allowed to participate in national government. While he was Governor of San Juan province Sarmiento engineered limited suffrage for educated women.[13]

Sarmiento's personal life was chaotic. In 1831 a young Chilean girl named María Jesús de Canto gave birth to his daughter, Faustina; upon María's death five years later Faustina went to live with her father. Several years later he became a father again by a married woman, Benita Martínez de Castro, whom he married upon her husband's death in 1848 and from whom he was separated in 1860. During his travels in the United States and Europe he had a series of affairs; perhaps the most passionate of these was with Ida Wickersham, the wife of a wealthy Chicagoan, which took place while Sarmiento was a guest in the Wickersham home in 1869. His most famous platonic relationship was with Aurelia Vélez Sarsfield, the daughter of the author of the Argentine Civil Code, who was unhappily married to Quiroga's secretary. Her correspondence with

Sarmiento became the center of her life. Several times a week for more than ten years they exchanged letters; he wrote to her about politics, literature and music, and she gave him advice about his personal affairs.

When he became Director of Education in 1856 Sarmiento at once sought out clever women to assist him. He appointed Juana Manso de Noronha head supervisor of the Board of Education for the province of Buenos Aires. She had been born in Buenos Aires in 1819, but her family, who were Unitarists, moved to Montevideo when she was a child. At the age of nineteen, she opened a girls' school which was so successful that the government of Uruguay asked her to found a public girls' school on that model.[14] Some time between 1837 and 1840 she and her family moved to Brazil, to Rio de Janeiro, where in 1841 she married Francisco de Saa Noronha, a well-known Portuguese violinist, with whom she then travelled extensively in Europe and the United States. At one point they settled in Philadelphia where Juana Manso de Noronha published poetry and toured the eastern United States with Elizabeth Peabody, Horace Mann's sister. Like Sarmiento, Juana Manso admired the North American system of public education. Sarmiento said that she alone in Argentina really understood his plans for public education and was selflessly devoted to them.[15]

From 1849 to 1853 Juana Manso lived in Rio, where she raised her three daughters, administered her girls' secondary school and published *The Women's Journal*, a periodical modeled on an English magazine of the same name. The *Journal* argued against discrimination against women and supported equal education for Latin American women. In 1853 Francisco de Saa Noronha mysteriously disappeared, leaving his wife without funds. She was forced to abandon her work in Brazil and return to Argentina where, on Sarmiento's appointment as National Minister of Education, she worked for the school system until her death in

1875. Her written work includes *A Brief History of the United Provinces of the Río de la Plata,* a valuable resource.

Sarmiento's appointment of Juana Manso to the important post of school supervisor for the province of Buenos Aires was unprecedented. In Argentina, middle-class women did not work, let alone take positions of authority over men. In addition, Juana Manso was a Protestant. Sarmiento said that his appointment of her came from his desire to lessen the influence of the "ignorant old women of the Beneficent Society."[16] He said this despite the fact that several of his sisters and cousins were active in the Society; his oldest sister Paula (1803-1899) founded a branch of the Society in the province of San Juan. The ladies of the Society, as might be expected, considered Sarmiento an arrogant, obnoxious heretic, and quarrelled with him for years about educational and religious issues. By the latter half of the nineteenth century, the Beneficent Society was no longer considered progressive. The attempts of these women to cling to the administration of all the charitable institutions in the state were seen as obstacles to the modernization of Argentine social systems.

In 1874 Sarmiento charged Emma Nicolay de Caprille (d. 1884) with founding a normal school for the National Department of Education. She and Sarmiento had met soon after her arrival in Buenos Aires in 1870 to become principal of the Domenical School under the administration of the Beneficent Society, and she was interested in his ideas about founding a normal school system on the North American model. She had been born in Poland and educated in Switzerland and Germany. In Florence she had married a penniless Frenchman; she and her husband had moved wherever she could get work as a teacher, since she was apparently the family breadwinner. Emma Nicolay de Caprille was described by one contemporary as "attractive, blue-eyed, curly haired, with charming manners . . . always elegantly dressed, always with a flower in her belt, always with a great dog, Huascar, preceding her . . ." She impressed the scholars of Buenos Aires with her apparent knowledge of Latin and Greek "and the literature of a dozen countries . . ."[17] She was a devout Catholic, but she said that "Sarmiento's progressive plans for women's education were the first step in the Argentine woman's struggle for liberation."[18] She administered Normal School Number One for the last ten years of her life.

Sarmiento had ambitious plans for the reformation of Argentine educational practices:

> The separation of the sexes [he said] in different schools derives from the . . . source which prevents women from participating in public acts. The cumulative result is . . . that a woman does not dare to show herself to be intelligent, nor to write . . . even a word, for it is the secret, unspoken belief that this is . . . indecent . . . Such are our customs, the remnants of barbarism, which we fail to notice because we are Latin American and nationalistic.[19]

In addition to co-education, Sarmiento wanted a national physical education program for girls; such a program already existed for boys. Sarmiento admired the Delsarte system, named after its creator, the Frenchman A.N. Delsarte (1811-1871), which combined calisthenics, dance and oral expression. Neither co-education nor physical education for girls was acceptable to Argentine society at that time, but Sarmiento's insistence on the reformation of education did not fall on deaf ears. In 1869 the Congress created a national normal school system, and in 1876 transferred control of girls' schools in the city and province of Buenos Aires from the Beneficent Society to the provincial government, on the grounds that the growing urban population needed a more sophisticated school system.

During his visits to the United States Sarmiento had developed a strong respect for the achievements of North American women, including Susan B. Anthony, whom he had heard speak in 1867. As a result he developed a plan to bring teachers from respected North American schools to establish normal schools in his country. From 1869 to 1886 sixty-five North American teachers, only four of whom were male, came to Argentina to help start more than thirty normal schools throughout the country.[20] They were given renewable one-year contracts at a higher rate of pay than in North America and compensation for their traveling expenses. Sarmiento required that the women, many of whom had been recruited by Mary Mann and Elizabeth Peabody, come from good homes and be physically attractive so that they could serve as role models for Argentine girls. Sarmiento admired particularly the pioneer spirit of the Midwest, where vocational training had been incorporated with regular classes. The Chicago public school system had impressed him particularly; in 1867 he had met Kate Newall Doggett, a prominent Chicagoan who was a suffragist and strong supporter of women's education; she recruited teachers for Sarmiento from Midwestern colleges and normal schools, happy, she said, to help bring Argentine women out of the seraglio.

George Stearns (1843-1916) was one of the four male recruits. Because he was a graduate of the University of Chicago and already had an international reputation as a teacher and educational innovator, Stearns was chosen by Sarmiento to found a model normal school at Paraná, Entre Ríos, where the Yankee teachers were to spend their first months in Argentina. Stearns and his wife Julia remained in the country for two years, establishing the curriculum at Paraná and training Argentine educators to run the school. It was at Paraná that the North Americans were to learn Spanish before being assigned to administrative and teaching posts in the provinces. Some teachers stayed on at Paraná for a few months to teach Argentine students. Only the most enlightened families enrolled their daughters at Paraná, since the school was co-educational and female students who came from other areas had to board there. Middle-class families had little choice if they wanted their daughters to receive more than the primary education customary for girls. The *colegios* and the Catholic universities were closed to females and were to remain so until the end of the century; secondary girls' schools were not established until at least the 1890s. Normal schools were free or required only token payment and since there was nowhere else for the middle-class girl to go for an education, from the beginning, half the students at Paraná were female. The curriculum was rigorous and difficult for Argentines of both sexes, who came, generally, insufficiently prepared.

From Paraná innovative educational philosophies were to spread throughout the country. The positivism of Auguste Comte, which put strong emphasis on the value of experience and on the sciences, combined with Darwinism to strongly influence Argentine thinking at about this time. Pedro Scalabrini (1849-1916), an Italian-born educator, philosopher and paleontologist, who was director of the normal school at Paraná from 1868 to 1890, is credited with introducing positivism into the Argentine normal school system. European and North American concepts were influential in Latin America in the nineteenth and twentieth centuries and especially in Argentina because of immigrants like Scalabrini who profoundly altered social attitudes. Scalabrini believed that in scientific observation lay the possibility of a new intellectual order in which the problems of the chaotic past could be solved. Through observation and experimentation, human behavior could be understood and modified. Children would choose to behave morally if they were taught "moral liberty" by enlightened teachers who would set them an example as hypocritical priests and ignorant pedagogues could not do. Children could learn only by example, from practical experience, and not by rote. They could learn positive behavior only from teachers who could earn their respect. Religious education Scalabrini held to be harmful, along with traditional Argentine teaching methods.

Customarily upper-class Argentine families sent at least one son to medical or law school, but these professional degrees were a status symbol rather than the key to a career because most young men did not practice their professions. This custom, which filled the country with uneducated lawyers and doctors, kept Argentina backward and in intellectual isolation, according to Scalabrini. He attacked, too, the Latin American disdain for manual labor, an Iberian attitude, saying that Argentine children should not be taught to believe that working with one's hands was only for the lower classes. The country was in desperate need of competent farmers, skilled workers, office personnel, health care workers and teachers. Practical education was the only solution.

Normalism was the normal school philosophy which relied on a positivist and evolutionary approach to learning; it was called by its practitioners "the science of progress and the science of man."[21] Normalists held that sociological "laboratories" like the one at Paraná, were the only places where Argentine children could be properly educated; they must first of all be removed from their home environments if they were to be helped to overcome the "natural deficiencies" of the native Argentine population. There was constant speculation among normal school students about whether their pupils in the model grade school at Paraná could overcome their predisposition to Spanish colonial backwardness. However, since most families either could not afford to or simply would not send their children to boarding school, and since most primary schools did not in any case have boarding facilities, this speculation was basically abstract. The teachers knew they would have to work with children who were living at home. For this reason both parents were assigned significant roles in child-rearing; the father in training the "intelligence" and the mother the "sentiments". Thus the education of women was important because of their strong influence on their children in at least the early years. An example of this attitude appears in an article called "The Education of Mothers" which was printed in a monthly educational journal founded in Paraná in 1885 and distributed by the National Department of Education. The writer makes the point that ignorant parents, mothers and fathers alike, resort to corporal punishment because they know no other way to act. Girls must take courses at normal schools in education for motherhood, so that they can learn how to care for small children scientifically, and learn that children must obey from respect and not from fear.[22]

All these plans hinged, of course, on the availability of trained teachers for the new normal schools. Sarmiento expected the North Americans to fill that gap; he had not foreseen the North American perception of Argentina as a dangerous place. The protracted civil wars and widespread anarchy had provided fertile ground for this perception. In 1869 Mary Elizabeth Gorman was the first North American teacher to arrive in Buenos Aires. She came from Akron, Ohio, and was assigned to be principal of a new normal school in San Juan province. But on the voyage from the States she had been told by North and South American passengers alike that the Argentine provinces were dangerous: the countryside was being terrorized by the *caudillos* and their bands of thugs. Consequently, much to Sarmiento's disgust, she refused to leave Buenos Aires. Angry, Sarmiento would not deal further with her. After she had been in the city for several weeks, and her money was running out, Juana Manso found a teaching post for her in the city. She remained in Buenos Aires for the rest of her life; in 1874 she married John Sewell, another North American expatriate. For a while she was involved in a dispute with the provincial government of San Juan which accused her of breaking her contract because of her refusal to go to the provinces, but this was resolved. She died in Buenos Aires in 1924.

A few months after Mary Gorman's arrival, three more North American teachers came to Buenos Aires and refused to go to the provincés, since their arrival had coincided with several political assassinations and the murder of innocent bystanders in the provinces of Entre Ríos, San Juan and Tucumán. The three women remained in Buenos Aires and started an infant school there; eventually Mary Gorman was to work with them. Sarmiento persevered, despite these disappointments, and in 1872, with the help of Kate Doggett, he was able to recruit several more teachers. The women who came at this time were less uneasy than their colleagues who had come earlier, because the provincial governments were beginning to control civic disorder and the situation in the interior was stabilizing. Most of these North American teachers were inspired by Sarmiento's ambitious plans for Argentine education; some had special educational interests of their own which they were eager to implement. And then of course there were some who had been lured by the relatively high salaries and the promise of adventure, and some who were simply looking for husbands. Twenty of the sixty-five women who came to Argentina to teach between 1869 and 1898 married there; only one married an Argentine. The others married North American and British Argentine residents. But whatever their reasons for coming, these women were earnest and dedicated enough to earn the respect of the communities in which they worked, and the lasting gratitude of the Argentine people. Although all the teachers believed in the separation of church and state and consequently in a secular school system, those North American teachers who were Catholic had a somewhat better reception than those who were Protestant, since people in the conservative interior distrusted non-Catholics.

All the teachers had had progressive educations in secular

normal schools in the United States where, after 1850, the influence of Catharine Beecher had been pervasive. Mrs. Beecher (1800-1878) was a strong supporter of practical domestic education for women; unlike many of the North American teachers she did not believe in woman suffrage, since she accepted a clear delineation between men's and women's spheres. Women's sphere she saw as the classroom and the home, a sphere that deserved respect. The backbone of female education for Catharine Beecher were courses in hygiene, nutrition, home economics and other domestic sciences, although she did not object to higher education for women.[23] One teacher who accepted Mrs. Beecher's philosophy was Mary Conway (1844-1903) who came from Boston to Argentina in 1877; she was principal of the normal school in Tucumán province for two years. She returned to Buenos Aires in 1879 and the following year founded the American School for daughters of foreigners and elite *porteño* families. Following Catharine Beecher's precepts, Mary Conway taught her pupils how to manage a household and give elegant dinner parties. Mrs. Beecher held that the home was the most important civilizing force in any society and women must, as the center of the home, develop themselves fully not only as mothers but as individuals. Thus along with domestic economy, the American School taught French, music and embroidery, and each girl was examined in physiology, hygiene and child care. Servants in Argentina, Mary Conway found, could not be relied upon, and, in any case, they could perform well only if the mistress of the house knew how to do everything herself. Further, the girls were taught to avoid flirtation and to be sincere and trustworthy. The school's motto was, "To be, not to seem". Mary Conway herself did not marry and she offered teaching as a worthy alternative to marriage. The school was successful: it became something of a social center and after the first year a waiting list developed. Mary Conway was prominent in social and cultural circles in Buenos Aires.

Another influential North American teacher was Mary Graham (1842-1906) who arrived in Argentina in 1879 and worked for twenty-seven years in the cities of Paraná and La Plata. In 1888 she founded the National Normal School of La Plata, and administered it until her death. She was a prohibitionist and a feminist who believed in co-education, although her school was for girls only. She objected strongly to the double standard of sexual conduct, believing that men should live according to the moral code which was imposed upon women. Like Mary Conway she emphasized practical education and encouraged her students to do philanthropic work in their spare time. Considered a fine role model for young girls, she talked often about the importance of personal sacrifice to achieve an education. In 1938, on the fiftieth anniversary of the founding of the National Normal School of La Plata, its name was changed to the Mary Graham Normal School. A poem, written by Cecilia Borja, was part of the celebration of the occasion:

> Mary O. Graham was the famous teacher
> Who founded this school with glory;
> Her clear, brilliant memory cannot
> Be erased by the years.
>
> In his forward-looking eagerness, Sarmiento
> Brought her from the United States,
> And with her soul and talent she knew
> How to make this land her own.
>
> Let us invoke her sanctified memory
> And we will still see her proud figure
> Rise like a ray of pure light
> From every hidden corner;
> Her soft walk, her penetrating look
> That can foretell the deepest thoughts.
> Her snow-white hair, her ivory skin,
> and on her lips, her great heart.
>
> She has the gift to guide wills,
> And the gift to attract hearts;
> And above all God gave her the

Ability to reach the truth.
Once, in an inspired phrase,
Someone said that she lived for education.
Today her spirit goes on radiating
Strength, optimism and good will.

CHORUS

Let your dear name always be
Mary O. Graham
Feeling, Strength, Idea,
Guiding light and symbol of good.[24]

Not all the teachers chose to spend their lives in Argentina. For instance, Ruth Wales came from Indiana in 1880 to teach chemistry, physics, drawing and early childhood education in normal schools in Mendoza and Rosario and, in 1883, in Paraná; she went home for good in 1884. Amy Wales, a relative of Ruth's, came from Chicago in 1882 and remained for two years, during which she established the Delsarte system of gymnastic instruction and physical fitness in the normal schools. Another Chicagoan, Abigail Nancy Ward, who was assistant principal of the Cottage Grove School before she arrived in Argentina in 1883, spent only a year in the country, but she established a model grade school attached to the Paraná normal school, an important accomplishment because it provided a place for students to practice-teach before they went on permanent assignments.

Some teachers contributed to Argentine community life. Jennie Howard (1845-1933) was an active member of the Columbia Club, which was important to North American residents of Buenos Aires. She had been assigned to teach in the provinces of Corrientes and Córdoba. After trying and failing to set up a nonsectarian normal school in Córdoba, she moved to Buenos Aires where she taught in the normal school, eventually becoming its director. She founded the American Women's Club for visiting Americans, and was a founding member of the Argentine branch of the Young Women's Christian Association. She remained in Buenos Aires and died there, one of the most popular of the "Yankee teachers".

Two other teachers active in the North American community were Clara and Frances Armstrong, from New York state. In 1882 Frances arrived in Córdoba to administer a national normal school; since the government had in the previous year passed the National Common Education Law which prohibited the teaching of religion in the public schools, she had expected her school to be secular. However Córdoba, which had been the religious center of Argentina, was a stronghold of traditional values: when Frances embarked on a program of physical education for girls without first notifying parents, and when she began early evening classes for working women, she incurred the wrath of Dr. Jerónimo Clara, the governor of Córdoba, who threatened to close the school unless she was dismissed at once. She did not respect Cordoban tradition, he said, which forbade the appearance of respectable women in the streets after dark without proper chaperones. The new teachers, he said, were Protestant heretics who were attempting to subvert the morality of Catholic students. The uproar was so great that Frances Armstrong was forced to leave Córdoba. Her sister Clara is remembered for having founded the Women's Exchange in Buenos Aires, for women of all nationalities resident or visiting.

Sarah Chamberlain Eccleston (1840-1916) also arrived in 1882 but had a somewhat more pleasant introduction to the Argentine school system. She wanted to start a kindergarten system based on the theories of Friedrich Wilhelm Froebel (1782-1852), the German educator. Sarah Eccleston, who came from the Winona Normal School in Minnesota, encountered some difficulty in persuading conservative parents that their children were ready at the age of four or five to learn how to cooperate with their peers, since Argentines believed that young children should spend their carefree early years at home with their parents and siblings. However, educated Argentines of the upper and middle classes in the urban areas of the littoral provinces accepted Sarah Eccleston's kindergarten plans because they were particularly interested in progressive ideas from Europe and North America. Newly arrived European immigrants also accepted the kindergarten theory; they believed fervently in education as a stepping-stone to successful lives. Thus more than twenty kindergarten societies were founded in Argentina, as well as community organizations of parents which worked with teachers and school administrators. Sarah Eccleston is known today as the grandmother of the Argentine kindergarten movement, just as Elizabeth Peabody is remembered as the grandmother of the movement in North America. Sarah Eccleston was also influential in the development of courses for girls in "mother science": early childhood education, hygiene, household management, and so on.

Many of the teachers were horrified to find primitive living accomodations, ramshackle school buildings and no instructional materials when they reached their assigned destinations. Frances Ward, arriving in Catamarca in 1884, burst into tears when she saw the dilapidated shack she was expected to live in. In that same year Jeanette Stevens and Theodora Gay arrived in Jujuy, a picturesque city in the foothills of the Andes, after a harrowing three week journey in bad weather, without accommodations along the way, and in constant terror of bandits who roamed the region. The people of Jujuy considered it a matter of pride to make these women comfortable. They repaired old buildings and built new ones. If these North American teachers did not try to institute sudden, radical change in rural customs, they were generally treated with great respect.

By the 1880s teaching in normal schools was considered suitable permanent employment for women, although not for men, who could not be expected to support families on such low pay. Men could go on to the University, which was effectively closed to women by custom, if not by law. Women, especially those who did not marry, could get better paying jobs in school administration and as school inspectors.

A network of women with similar interests grew in Argentina as normal school teachers in isolated provincial towns developed warm friendships with one another and kept in touch when they were separated. In the latter part of the nineteenth century articles proliferated in journals and magazines about women's education, the improvement of women's social and economic situation, their function in the home and their lives in general. European immigrants, who were working in health services, government and primary and secondary education, translated European and North American feminist literature into Spanish. As a group, immigrants thought more about social progress than native Argentines, and were more interested in women's education. After 1890 seventy percent of the normal schools were for women, and by 1905 over half of the students at the college preparatory National Girls School Number One in Buenos Aires came from immigrant families.[25]

Women of Buenos Aires edited two journals: *The Home Movement* (*La Columna del Hogar*), which carried articles by normal school teachers and child specialists, and *Advancement* (*Adelanto*), dedicated to Argentine primary and secondary schools and female teachers, many of whom wrote for it. *Advancement* advocated increased instruction in mathematics and science and a quickening of the pace of instituting equal education for women. Equality here meant something like "separate but equal", since no one asked that boys and girls receive the same kind of education. Women's roles in life were thought to require a different kind of education from men's, although women's education should still be first-class. The founders of these two magazines also founded the first women's library in Buenos Aires.[26]

Most of the people admired by the writers of *The Normalist, The Home Movement* and *Advancement* were foreigners; among the few Argentines was Domingo Sarmiento who was credited with bringing civilization to Argentina; his Yankee teacher plan, they felt, had begun to lift the country out of "Hispanic backwardness".[27] The teachers supported open immigration, which was populating the pampas region. Generations of students were taught that Argentina did not really become a civilized country until its culture had absorbed foreign influences. This attitude was codified in textbooks produced by the teachers at Paraná and was strongly attacked by Nationalists in the 1930s and '40s, who accused the textbook writers of breeding self-hatred in Argentine schoolchildren. However, despite the inevitable swings of action and reaction in the body politic, the teachers and administrators of the national normal school system continued to respect the work of Sarmiento's North American teachers who made a substantial contribution toward lowering the illiteracy rate in Argentina from two-thirds of the population in 1896 to less than one-third in 1914.[28]

During the 1870s and 1880s trade schools were run, as a rule, by Italian, French, British and Spanish community organizations. A few small trade schools and commercial training institutions, each with rarely more than fifteen or twenty students, were operated by Catholic charities. The national government was slow to recognize the real growing need for skilled and semi-skilled workers. In 1896, during the presidency of Luis Sáenz Peña, the National Department of Education opened a manual training school in Buenos Aires for primary schoolgirls. For women the Crafts and Service Institute offered courses in lacemaking, dress design, bookbinding, glovemaking and other crafts. Laundering and ironing were taught, but they were not popular with students.[29] There was a constant demand for laundry workers, but the pay was low and working conditions were not satisfactory. Low pay was characteristic for most work done by women. The 1914 national census found that the overwhelming majority of employed women did piecework in clothing factories or sweatshops, or worked at home in what was called the letting-out system; the latter were paid even less than the former.[30] Nevertheless it was thought practical to train women for work they could do at home. The government considered women's labor of marginal economic importance, even though by 1914 women constituted twenty-two percent of the Argentine work force.[31] There was little organized demand for adequate vocational training; teachers in the trade and commercial schools for women emphasized the science of motherhood and what could be called "intelligent patriotism". It is conceivable that these teachers themselves lacked sufficient training to teach the necessary skills. However, despite these drawbacks, the only serious practical training in the country was provided by public and vocational schools.

By the 1880s Buenos Aires had become a major center of banking and commerce in South America; because clerical workers were urgently needed, several private and public secretarial schools for women were opened. In 1912 the government founded a co-educational commercial high school where men were trained for jobs like paralegal work and women were taught only basic clerical skills. Women were severely hampered in any case by civil as well as social discrimination. It must be remembered that married women could not sign contracts or make legal or economic decisions without their husbands' permission, and all women were forbidden to participate in any way in court actions, even as witnesses. Paralegal training would thus be wasted on them.

In 1905 the National Girls' High School Number One opened, the first of a series of secondary schools established to prepare women for university; it was staffed by normal and private school teachers. Academic standards were high and attendance at the school conferred status on the girls and their families. Courses included advanced science and mathematics, along with early childhood education, since the teachers wanted "infant science" to be elevated academically. Although individual achievement was not denigrated, emphasis was put on the importance of home and community responsibilities and on the necessity of avoiding egoism.

By 1910 Argentina had an international reputation for having the best educational system in Latin America, and was the only Latin American country, with the exception of Uruguay, morally and financially committed to the education of women.[32] Although foreign teachers went to other Latin American countries — North Americans to Mexico and Germans to Chile, for instance — the dissemination of foreign ideas was greatest in Argentina. Prominent educators visited the National Girls' High School: in 1907 Maria Montessori came from Italy to lecture on kindergarten methods there and at the University of Buenos Aires.

The establishment of university preparatory schools for women and the opening to them of the doors of the University, marked the real beginning of the feminist movement in Argentina. In 1905 only eleven women had been graduated from the University of Buenos Aires. Between 1905 and 1910 twenty-five women had completed graduate and undergraduate courses. All twenty-five practiced professions, in medicine, social work, education or science,[33] and all became strong advocates of women's social and economic advancement. They donated their time to the National Girls High School to inform young women about what they would encounter after graduation and to upgrade the School where they could. Some of them even advocated the vote for women, an extreme view for Argentine women at that time.

Alicia Moreau de Justo, one of the founders of Argentine feminism, had said that she and Paulina Luisi, a Uruguayan educator, decided early in their lives that education for women must come before their civil and political equality. They had discerned this pattern in other countries and they believed that feminism had to evolve in a logical way from one stage to another.

Notes

[1]Domingo Sarmiento, *Life in the Argentine Republic in the Days of the Tyrants; or Civilization and Barbarism* (NY: Hafner, 1971), p. 283.

[2]Antonio Dellepiane, *El testamento de Rosas*, pp. 58-65.

[3]Sosa de Newton, *Diccionario biográfico*, p. 317.

[4]Sosa de Newton, p. 168.

[5]Percas, "Women Poets", p. 12.

[6]Percas, p. 13.

[7]Mörner, *Race Mixture*, p. 134.

[8]Argentine Republic, "Censo escolar nacional" (B.A.: 1884).

[9]L. S. Rowe, "Educational Progress in the Argentine Republic and Chile" in *Report of the Commissioner of Education for the Year Ending June 30, 1909* (Washington, D.C.: U.S. Gov't Printing Office, 1909).

[10]For information on Sarmiento, see Frances G. Crowley, *Sarmiento, Teacher of the Americas* (NY: Twayne Publ., 1972); *Obras completas de Domingo Sarmiento* (B.A.: Editorial del Día, 1948-1956); Alice Houston Luiggi, "Some Letters of Sarmiento and Mary Mann," HAHR, (May, 1952); Sarmiento *Life.*

[11]Alice Houston Luiggi, *Sixty-Five Valiants* (Gainesville: Univ. of Fla Press, 1965), p. 6.

[12]Luiggi, "Some Letters", pp. 187-212; *La Prensa*, 25 July, 1919, p. 10; June Hahner, "Feminism, Women's Rights and the Suffrage Movement in Brazil", LARR 15, No. 1 (1980), 65-112.

[13]Crowley, p. 135.

[14]Sosa de Newton, *Diccionario*, p. 220.

[15]Luiggi, *Sixty-Five Valiants*, p. 29.

[16]*Ibid*, pp. 26-28.

[17]*Ibid*, p. 114.

[18]*Unión y Labor* 3, No. 32 (1912), 2-3.

[19]Crowley, *Sarmiento*, p. 136.

[20]Most of the information following comes from Jennie E. Howard, *In Distant Climes and Other Years* (BA: American Press, 1931) and Luiggi, *Sixty-Five Valiants.*

[21]*El Normalista*, 1 Nov., 1888, p. 8.

[22]Mariana Gilbert Bergez, "La educación de las madres", *El Normalista*, 1 Dec., 1888, pp. 3-7.

[23]See Kathryn Kish Sklar, *Catharine Beecher: A Study in American Domesticity* (NY: Norton, 1973).

[24]La escuela normal nacional Mary Olstine Graham, *Obra escrito en celebración de su cincuentenario, 1888-1938* (La Plata: 1938), p. 53.

[25]Luis Herrera, "Liceo nacional de señoritas de la capital," *Boletín de la Instrucción Pública*, 12 (May, 1913), 89.

[26]Elvira López, "El movimiento feminista", Diss. Univ. of B.A. 1901, pp. 74-80.

[27]*El Normalista*, (Nov., 1888), p. 2.

[28]Scobie, *Argentina*, p. 154.

[29]Little, "Education, Philanthropy and Feminism", p. 240.

[30]*Censo (Tercer) Nacional de la República Argentina, 1914*, pp. 395-397.

[31]See Hollander, "Women in the Political Economy," Chaps. 1 and 2.

[32]Anna Macías, "Felipe Carrillo Puerto and Women's Liberation in Mexico," in *Latin American Women: Historical Perspectives*, ed. Asunción Lavrin, (Westport, CT: Greenwood Press, 1978), pp. 254-285; Cynthia Jefferson Little, "Moral Reform and Feminism: A Case Study," *Journal of Interamerican Studies and World Affairs* 17 no 4 (1975), 386-397; Catharine Manny Paul, "Amanda Labarca H.: Educator of the Women of Chile," Diss. NYU 1967.

[33]Argentine Republic, Ministerio del Trabajo, Oficina Nacional de la Mujer, Dirección Nacional de Recursos Humanos, *Evolución de la mujer en las profesiones liberales en Argentina*, años 1900-1965, 2nd ed. BA, 1970, p. 82.

4

The National Council of Women In Argentina

> Those who are not yet in agreement with the advanced ideas that proclaim women's emancipation do not have to be afraid. Our society is not prepared for this great evolution; nor could our sweet and essentially restrictive customs be molded to a new phase that demands force, independence and a resolved and manly spirit which without a doubt would snatch away the poetic halo from young Argentine ladies.
>
> We will wait for that transcendent change, if the law of progress imposes it as necessary. We hope that among us education is established which enhances, which obliges respect and consideration for women, which places her in a superior sphere where unjust criticism and wicked jokes do not reach her.[1]
>
> Carolina de Jaimes
> "Una hermosa sociedad
> feminista", 1901

In 1898 twenty women's charitable and philanthropic organizations sponsored a Women's Exposition at the Teatro Colón in Buenos Aires, to display the accomplishments of Argentine women in fine and decorative arts, crafts and charitable activities. This Exposition was a direct result of the Columbian Exposition in Chicago in 1893, where, in the Woman's Building, nations in all parts of the world displayed work by women in art, medicine, science, crafts, philanthropy and education over the past four hundred years.[2] Argentina was not among the few Latin American countries which sent exhibits to the Woman's

Building. Dr Ernesto Quesada, a professor of philosophy and history at the University of Buenos Aires who served as advisor to the Beneficent Society, had been embarrassed by his country's neglect of this impressive opportunity to demonstrate the accomplishments of its women. He had suggested the Women's Exposition as a partial atonement for that regrettable lapse.

However, the displays in Buenos Aires disappointed Dr Quesada. There were no exhibits of highly skilled crafts like lacemaking, and no point was made of Argentine women's advances in liberal education. Dr Quesada thought that too much emphasis was placed at the Exhibition on the training of poor immigrants to become domestic servants or seamstresses. Why were there no demonstrations of real Argentine talents for cooking, painting and music? Dr Quesada believed that the women of his country could compete culturally with women from France, Britain and North America. He was forced to conclude that they put together so poor a showing because they lacked confidence in themselves; Argentine culture had imbued them with a sense of inferiority. He did not want female emancipation that would masculinize Argentine women or reverse the roles of the sexes, but it seemed to him obvious that reform was necessary if Argentines were to hold their own, as they deserved to do, with women of Western nations. The women of his country, he said, should use their organizational talents to pressure the government for more female technical education. They should imitate women's organizations like the International Council of Women and the New England Women's Clubs to bring more enlightened attitudes to Argentina. Unmarried women should have the opportunity to work without threatening male employment: department store jobs, secretarial work, nursing — these would give women useful employment without outraging society, and this must be done if Argentina were to become a modern nation.[3]

At the opening of the Women's Exposition, Dr Quesada called on normally conservative Argentine Catholic women for support. His speech reflected the concern of the government, the Church and the Beneficent Society about increasing infanticide, child neglect and abuse, and prostitution in the littoral provinces. Rapid economic expansion and urbanization were raising the spectre of public disorder. Thousands of immigrants were flocking to find work in a politically unstable country with fluctuating economic cycles and sporadic unemployment.[4] Dr Quesada urged all classes of Argentines to unite to create work for the immigrants, to obviate the danger of serious political unrest which could occur through the spread of foreign ideologies.[5] He concluded his talk by asking the President of the Republic, Julio Roca, to encourage the organization of women's clubs that would work to move Argentina into the future in a progressive and orderly manner.

One women's group had already approached the Argentine government for help: the International Council of Women (ICW) had grown out of the Women's Congresses at the Paris Exposition of 1889, to which May Wright Sewell had been the only North American delegate from the National Council of Women, founded in 1888 in Washington, D.C., by suffragists. In Paris Mrs Sewell and other feminists had planned the formation of the International Council of Women. In 1896 Isabel King, a North American resident of Buenos Aires, had unsuccessfully requested the government's co-operation in the formation of an Argentine branch of the ICW.[6]

Mrs King, one of the first group of teachers recruited by Sarmiento, had moved to Buenos Aires province, after her initial assignment in the interior, to become a respected normal school administrator. On her retirement, she chose to remain in Argentina, maintaining a lively correspondence with educators and social reformers in the United States. In 1893 she went to Chicago to attend the ICW meeting at the Columbian Exposition, having received an invitation from May Wright Sewell. She addressed the membership and when she was asked about the feasibility of forming branches of the organization in South America, replied that this was possible only in Argentina and Uruguay, where the population was predominantly European in origin and reasonably progressive in attitude.[7]

On her return to Argentina, Mrs King followed the established procedure of the ICW by asking the government and the wife of the president to sponsor a National Council of Women organization in Buenos Aires, and by contacting the charity organizations as well. She was either ignored or rebuffed. She decided then to contact directly the few professional women in the city. Accordingly Jean Thompson Raynes, an Englishwoman active in English-speaking women's cultural and philanthropic organizations, received an invitation to the second International Congress of the ICW to be held in London in 1899. Mrs Raynes attended the Congress, accompanied by Cecilia Grierson (1850-1934), a physician who was to become a leading Argentine feminist.

Dr Grierson's maternal grandparents had been among the first Scottish immigrants in Argentina; her father had come from England to farm in the province of Entre Ríos, where he was killed in a political uprising. Her mother taught in the local primary school; all her female relatives were teachers and midwives in Entre Ríos, where they introduced hygienic methods of childbirth and significantly lowered the incidence of infant mortality.[8] At the age of fifteen, after assisting her mother in the primary school, Cecilia Grierson went to study at the normal school in Buenos Aires; she went from there to the University of Buenos Aires and graduated from medical school in 1889. She had encountered ridicule and emotional isolation because she was at that time the only woman at the University, and she had to fight a long legal battle to be allowed to practice medicine.[9] Thus her awareness of the need for revision of Argentine attitudes toward women was based on bitter experience.

Cecilia Grierson dedicated her career to the improvement of the lives of Argentine women, founding a professional nursing school and the first association of obstetricians and obstetrical nurses, and teaching obstetrics and physical therapy. By 1899 her reputation, as a doctor and a worker for women's education, was secure.

At the ICW conference in London, Dr Grierson was greatly impressed by the democratic attitudes of European elite women, which contrasted strongly with the class consciousness of Argentine charity volunteers. The membership appeared to heed the ICW's motto which was the Golden Rule: "Do unto others as you would have others do unto you." She was impressed also by the discussions, which dealt with philosophy, education, temperance, women in industry, the interests of professional women, women's clubs, legal and political matters and the question of a single moral standard for both sexes which would put an end to legalized prostitution.[10]

In her enthusiasm, Dr Grierson, who was made an honorary vice-president of the ICW, committed herself to form a branch of the Council in Argentina. Although the ICW and their affiliated NCW branches were suffragist organizations, with Susan B. Anthony and Elizabeth Cady Stanton among their founders, Cecilia Grierson believed that any branch of the organization in Argentina must put emphasis on awakening women to the need to work for social and moral reform, rather than on votes for women, since there was not yet even universal male suffrage in the country. She discussed all this in London with such notable women as Clara Barton, the founder of the International Red Cross, and the Countess of Aberdeen, an influential philanthropist and worker for reform.

As a result, Dr Grierson returned to Argentina convinced that simple charity as it existed in the country was not enough. A more sophisticated approach to the problems of society was needed, including humane treatment of women and children, progressive education and greater equality between the sexes. She began a campaign to enlist support for the formation of a National Council of Women in Argentina from the government, the press and women's charities. But the idea of a national organization of women dedicated to social reform and with strong ties to Europe and North America struck terror into the Argentine soul. The press did not like the ICW's suffragist stand and Dr Grierson could not convince them that suffrage was not a goal for Argentina, and that member organizations were allowed by the ICW to deal independently with controversial issues.[11] Some women said frankly that they did not want to belong to such an organization because they could not bear the thought of being criticized by men.[12]

Finally, after several frustrating months, Dr Grierson succeeded in winning over Alvina Van Praet de Sala, President of the Beneficent Society and a member of an old landowning family in the province of Buenos Aires, whose mother had joined the Beneficent Society in 1865, and who was influential enough to persuade representatives of thirty-three Argentine charitable and cultural organizations to attend the first meeting of the National Council of Women in September, 1900. Among the elegant philanthropists and lovers of literature were a few middle-class professional women.[13]

At this meeting it was decided that the NCW would function as an umbrella organization for women's clubs and philanthropic groups. Each member was to pay a token annual fee and to try and recruit both organizations and individual women. Alvina Van Praet de Sala was elected president and Cecilia Grierson became one of five vice-presidents making up an executive committee that would decide the form and content of monthly meetings. It was hoped that each member would have a voice in the planning of programs, so that no one's pet cause would pre-dominate. Everyone agreed that home and family were the main interests of females; therefore both "The Improvement of the Home" and "The Future Elevation of Woman" were broad enough topics to attract various women's groups. It was agreed that their goal should be the education of women so that they could win society's respect and fulfil their roles in life. It was agreed also that men were more intelligent and rational than women, but that women were morally superior to men.

In a letter to May Wright Sewell, Alvina Van Praet de Sala explained that the thirty-three organizations and one hundred and twenty-five individuals who made up the Argentine NCW were repelled by what seemed to them the anti-religious nature of the feminist movements in the United States and Britain. The use of the alarming word "feminism" would have to be avoided in Argentina. In order to shield the new organization from accusations of atheism, President Van Praet de Sala decreed that a priest be present at all general meetings. It was pointed out to her, to no avail, that Argentina had long ago embraced religious tolerance. Cecilia Grierson said that it should be remembered that President Rivadavia, one of the country's greatest leaders, had been a Mason; if he were alive he would not see the necessity for the government-sponsored NCW to refuse to meet without the blessing of the Church.[14]

This was just one of the many points on which Alvina Van Praet de Sala and Cecilia Grierson differed: from the beginning their personal values conflicted. For a while they were able to compromise. Alvina Van Praet de Sala deferred to Dr Grierson on policy questions because the doctor's journey to London and her honorary vice-presidency gave her status — for the first months, at least. In her turn Dr Grierson accepted President Van Praet de Sala's social arrangements. The NCW meetings were, after all, partly social gatherings, although much business was transacted too. The programs included concerts and poetry readings, as well as educational sessions in which members were informed about ICW activities around the world. The NCW published a magazine which contained international correspondence translated into Spanish by bilingual and polylingual members.

But before the organization could celebrate its first anniversary, real conflict erupted between the President and the doctor. Alvina Van Praet de Sala, who, as President of the Beneficent Society was accustomed to being treated with a certain amount of deference, wanted her name to appear on the cover of the NCW periodical. It was she who had helped bring member organizations under the umbrella of the NCW and it was she who through her connections had been able to convince the Rural Society to donate a meeting room. She and her friends agreed that she should be credited for her accomplishments; in addition the use of her name could only enhance the reputation of the organization.

Cecilia Grierson and the other professional women looked upon this as an attempt at self-aggrandizement. They felt that no officers should promote themselves at the Council's expense. This argument was incomprehensible to the Van Praet de Sala faction, which constituted the majority of the membership. The President's name was printed on the cover of the magazine and appears on the cover to this day.

At meetings NCW members learned about the varied work being done by women's organizations in trade and technical schools, in asylums, orphanages and hospitals. Special membership drives were held in the provinces where it had always been know that recruitment would be difficult. After some initial misunderstandings (one philanthropic organization in Córdoba wrote to ask the NCW for funds to build an orphanage; the NCW explained that it did not dispense financial assistance), women in San Juan, Córdoba and Mendoza joined, maintaining correspondence with headquarters; Buenos Aires dominated the organization. Nevertheless women's libraries were built in Rosario and La Plata, and courses were given there in secretarial and other vocational skills, in first aid, child care and languages. By 1905 three hundred individuals and one hundred societies had been recruited to the NCW. At every meeting announcements were made of new members. It remained necessary to reassure members and prospective members that the Council was not radical, atheist and/or suffragist. Carolina de Jaimes, one of the five vice-presidents, had made the point that feminism in Argentina had no connection with suffragism. In Argentina women were working toward future civil and political progress; the NCW in Argentina, she said, would never demand woman suffrage.

The differences between Alvina Van Praet de Sala and Cecilia Grierson, or between the philanthropists and the professional women, were deep and real. The professional women had joined the NCW expecting that it would take a strong stand on solutions to Argentine women's social and economic problems. But they found instead what they perceived to be a superficial and self-congratulatory approach to women's problems. In 1901 Gabriela de Coni (1866-1906) a leftist social worker and writer who was acting as press secretary to the NCW, resigned, saying she had better things to do than sip tea with society ladies.[15] This was an open acknowledgement of a serious rift. When women like Gabriela de Coni attempted to address the membership or write articles for the NCW periodical, they encountered criticism and even censorship from the President and her allies, who at the same time fended off inquiries from the ICW about activities of the Argentine branch by responding that although, because of their European roots, Argentine and Uruguayan women were more advanced in many ways than their Latin American sisters, they were still not

up to the standards of the majority of the member organizations of the ICW; they were not yet ready to try to effect
changes in the Civil Code or to discuss suffrage. They
needed time. When the ICW asked for information about
work in education and other areas, the Argentine executive
board sent them a short history of the Beneficent Society
and Argentine philanthropy.[16]

Dr Grierson was so annoyed at this inadequate response
that she herself in 1902 began an intensive study of the Civil
Codes so that the ICW would see that Argentine women
were capable of preparing a proper report, complete with
statistics. The report, completed in 1906, made the point
that only widows and single women had civil rights in
Argentina. Married women had the status of children that
they had had under colonialism. Dr. Grierson agreed with
the majority of the NCW that the Civil Code needed revision before work for suffrage could begin; but it was not
easy to convince the membership even of the need for civil
reform. For instance, many members rejected the idea of
legal divorce, because they feared for the financial future of
women and children if men were allowed to divorce their
wives. The issue of economic independence for both married and unmarried women was a frequent topic of NCW
discussions.[17]

By 1902 the professional women were discontented
enough to announce the formation of a new organization,
to be called the Argentine Association of University Wom-
en. Such an organization, which would address the needs of
women university graduates and working women was, they
said, needed now, as Argentina moved into a more progressive era: the "prejudices of the pampa", stemming from
Hispanic colonialism, were giving way to "pampa secu-
larism" because of European immigration. Among the
thirty women who founded the new organization were
Elvira López, her sister Ernestina López de Nelson, Ana
Pintos, Elvira Rawson de Dellepiane, Sara Justo, Cecilia

Grierson and Petrona Eyle, all of whom held advanced degrees: two in philosophy, four in medicine and one in dentistry. The AAUW was inaugurated at a dinner from which men and the press were excluded, and then the AAUW joined the NCW with the declared intention of liberalizing it. They announced that their aim was not to revolutionize the social order, but to provide moral support for professional women, and to preach rational feminism. They planned to do social work in a new AAUW center, which was to be open to all women free of charge.[18]

As could be expected, Alvina Van Praet de Sala decried what she called the unattractive "reclusive" attitude of the new group. A few months later, when an organization of female freethinkers which called itself God, Country and Science, applied for membership in the NCW, the President refused them. Their President, Carolina de Argerich, from a prominent *porteño* family, protested that her group was basically scholarly, without revolutionary intentions; they wanted only to promote the infusion of rationality into religion. Alvina Van Praet de Sala responded that free thinking fomented anti-clericalism and she did not want so disruptive a group in the NCW. In fact ICW rules forbade presidents of affiliate organizations the right to make arbitrary decisions about membership applications. All women's organizations had the right to join unless they had openly been organized for the purpose of violent overthrow of the existing government.[19] Cecilia Grierson accused the President of rejecting God, Country and Science because she resented younger women who had more education than her generation. But the European and North American leadership of the ICW wanted the Argentines to serve as liaison between them and women in other Latin American countries; they allowed President Van Praet de Sala's decision to stand. Argentina had, after all, the most advanced social service network in Latin America. If the Argentines were offended and refused to cooperate with women in Chile, Uruguay and Brazil who wished to form Councils, these organizations might never develop.

In 1903, on the third anniversary of the founding of the Argentine NCW, the ICW executive committee congratulated the women of their only Latin American affiliate on their achievements. The government of Argentina had recognized the NCW as an official organization which could represent the nation at international conferences and the Argentine Congress had appropriated funds for travel to these conferences by NCW delegates. This was something which had not been accomplished by European or North American women. President Julio Roca (1898-1904) responded to Alvina Van Praet de Sala's request for government aid because he wanted his government to project a good image abroad. In 1909, under the administration of José Figueroa (1906-1910) the Congress gave the NCW ten thousand pesos to help support their library and its evening classes.[20]

On occasion the ICW expressed some irritation with the Argentine organization. In 1904 the ICW requested that the Argentines stop sending all their correspondence in Spanish, since accepted practice, with which all Councils complied, was that international correspondence was conducted in English, French or German. The Argentine Council had many bilingual and polylingual members but the President did not ask for a program of translation. Throughout Alvina Van Praet de Sala's tenure, French and English translations of NCW activities appeared only occasionally. Although she had a reputation for efficiency, she apparently felt no pressure to respond promptly to ICW requests nor to communicate closely with them. It took, for instance, a full year and a half for the Argentines to reply to the ICW's policy of moral support for the work of the International Arbitration Committee which was attempting to end the Boer War.[21] Emma Willard, the American reformer and temperance worker, had introduced the reso-

All of the photographs are from the collection of Archivo Gráfico in the Archivo General de la Nacion, Buenos Aires, and are reproduced with permission. The archives do not always contain accurate and specific infomation about the people and the dates in these photographs.

Argentine Association for Women's Suffrage

Raquel Camaña (left) with Dr Julieta Lanteri de Renshaw

Nicolas Repetto and his wife
Fenia Chertkoff de Repetto
in her studio.

Dr Sara Justo (on left),
with an unidentified woman
and Dr Cecilia Grierson
(on right).

Dr Elvira Rawson de Dellepiane with some of her children. Note the amusing result of positioning the youngest child on the pedestal table and the boy to the left sitting on a stuffed animal.

Testing the rules: in Buenos Aires prior to universal suffrage, Dr Julieta Lanteri de Renshaw (granted citizenship in 1911) presents herself at a voting center for an election from which all women were barred from voting.

Alfonsina Storni at a poetry reading.

Dr Cecilia Grierson,
the first woman
medical doctor in Argentina.

Victoria Ocampo

Dr Elvira Rawson
de Dellepiane

Dr Sara Justo, March 15, 1920

Dr Alicia Moreau
de Justo
delivering a speech
in 1952

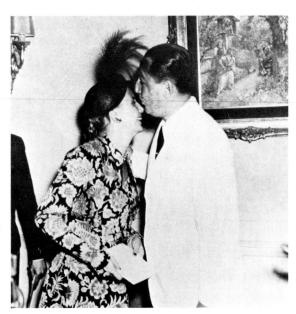

Juan and
Eva Perón, 1951

Political rally of women members of a Peronist neighborhood unit after
September 1947, when women were given the vote.

Evita, March 1950

Mourners in Buenos Aires, watching the funeral procession for
Eva Perón, July 26, 1952.

lution to emphasize the commitment of the ICW to peace everywhere in the world. But it was completely out of the question for the majority of the Argentine membership to hold a demonstration in a public place. Several months elapsed before President Van Praet de Sala sent her apologetic refusal to this request. She asked the ICW to forgive her slowness to respond: the women of Argentina, she said, did not have the energy and experience to answer promptly all the ICW's requests. She appealed for understanding of Latin culture, to which haste was alien. In this way she avoided action and confrontation; she relied on the clever women in the international organization to understand her meaning.[22]

Alvina Van Praet de Sala was not averse to action in some areas. She was devoted to working for the protection of pregnant working women. She wanted these women excused from work for two weeks before and two weeks after they gave birth. Although no one argued against the importance of maternity leave, the professional women in the NCW believed that the President's plan was not far-reaching enough. Cecilia Grierson drew up an alternative plan which called on the government to provide funds for extensive maternity leave and benefits, including social services. Because the President was sincerely interested in the plight of pregnant women, Dr Grierson and Elvira Rawson were able to convince her to endorse their plan. She did this, and the subsequent bill went to the Argentine Congress where, in 1906, it was rejected by a conservative majority.

In 1908 the Congress rejected another bill proposed by the NCW in conjunction with three other philanthropies: the Association against the White Slave Trade [headed for many years by Petrona Eyle (1866-1945), one of the first physicians to be graduated from the University of Buenos Aires, in 1893]; the Jewish Association for the Protection of Girls and Women, an international organization; and the Young Women's Christian Association founded by resident

Englishwomen in 1896. These organizations worked to find jobs and suitable lodgings for immigrant girls, against the white slave trade, which was centered at that time in Buenos Aires, and against the legalization of prostitution. The legislation which was presented to the Congress in 1908 would have made possible the prosecution of procurers.[23]

As the NCW tried to approach these social problems, the split in philosophy and attitude between the philanthropists and the professional women continued to cause friction. The majority, represented by the President, wanted to continue to support the work of the Beneficient Society and similar philanthropic organizations and the NCW's evening education classes. Dr Grierson and the AAUW considered these programs inadequate. They wanted a training school for domestic and skilled work, with rigorous up-to-date methods that would enable the trainees to be competitive in the job market; job training was the only realistic way, they felt, to keep women from prostitution. Dr Grierson wanted teachers from the Argentine Association of Nurses and Masseuses, with which she was connected, to staff the prospective school. And she proposed the establishment of a program of evening classes taught by competent teachers to train poor women for a variety of work apart from domestic service.

Alvina Van Praet de Sala was at first reluctant to accept this program; she pleaded inadequate funds. However, Dr Grierson was persistent and in the end won the day. Just a few months after the plan was presented to the executive committee, the NCW announced the opening of the School for Domestic and Technical Training.[24]

A year later, in 1907, the ICW expressed some concern to Buenos Aires about the commitment of the Argentine NCW to woman suffrage. The Argentines were asked to send delegates to an international suffrage conference and to take a position on the establishment of an organization which would work, independent of the ICW, only on international woman suffrage. The Argentines responded, as they had before, that the civil status of women in Argentina was so primitive that any discussion of suffrage would be premature. At the moment there was a bill before the Argentine Congress, presented by Socialists, which would give women some property rights and rights over their children; the NCW wanted to see how this bill fared before approaching the Congress about woman suffrage. It was extremely important that married women be allowed to control their own money and their own children. The Argentine NCW pointed out that it was a little company of women put on earth to fight the forces of evil. Surely, they said, if they trusted in God and went on fighting a little longer, they could find the strength to address dangerous projects like suffrage.[25]

Dr Grierson agreed that civil rights should take precedence over suffrage, but she and other AAUW women objected strongly to what they considered the childish, self-pitying tone of the response, which they felt would humiliate them in the eyes of the ICW. As dissension mounted, Dr Grierson attempted to bypass the President's authority and take all issues in contention directly to the philanthropic organizations which comprised the NCW, including the Beneficent Society, of which, of course, Alvina Van Praet de Sala was President. Dr Grierson openly asked these women to push the NCW to agitate for social and moral reform. Her mission, she believed, was to "enlighten" these ladies about the importance of change, to force them to move with the times. But the philanthropic ladies politely declined to be persuaded by the doctor's missionary zeal. They pointed out that they were philanthropists, not social workers. Social workers might be political; they were not. In their opinion it was unwise to mix politics and charity. And they refused to be swayed.

The simmering contention between Dr Grierson and the

President burst into flames over the centenary celebrations for the founding of the Republic, which were scheduled for 1910. The government planned various impressive activities, and allocated funds to the NCW to publicize the contributions of women to the public welfare. The NCW planned to hold a conference in 1910 as their share in the festivities, in which various women's groups would discuss their work and meet with one another socially. Immediately a division of opinion sprang up about this conference program. Cecilia Grierson denounced the NCW plan as insensitive to the pressing needs of Argentine women. In the resulting heat of battle Dr Grierson resigned from the NCW; the AAUW and other like-minded women's organizations withdrew from the NCW and announced plans to hold their own conference in 1910.

In retaliation Alvina Van Praet de Sala withdrew all funding from the School for Domestic and Technical Education and stripped Dr Grierson, somewhat after the fact, of her honorary vice-presidency. The President made clear her intention to run the NCW as she ran the Beneficent Society, without dissident and uncontrollable elements. Her support was strong.

Dr Grierson's response was a book, published in 1910, called *The Decadence of the Argentine NCW*, in which she said that the majority of the membership behaved childishly because they were uneducated and consequently had no real confidence in themselves. They were used to depending upon others and could not carry tasks to completion; they did not think for themselves and displayed constant public self-denigration. Some were genuinely passive; in others outward passivity cloaked ferocious aggressiveness. In the latter case, she was unquestionably referring to Alvina Van Praet de Sala who, she believed, had a personal vendetta against her because she, Dr Grierson, had exposed the President's shallowness and immaturity.

By 1910 the NCW had a membership of one thousand

women, most of whom, despite their reluctance to enter the political arena, were dedicated to work for the improvement of all women's lives.[26] The inevitable split between the philanthropists and the political activists in the NCW mirrored to some extent the tensions of Argentine society from 1900 to 1910, when there were labor strikes and general social and economic turmoil.[27]

Some women found it possible to continue their relationship with the NCW while at the same time forming new organizations with more distinct political goals. Perhaps the most interesting of these women was Elvira Rawson de Dellepiane who, in 1905, with the help of the AAUW, founded the Feminist Center for those women's groups interested in political and social reform. Although she was also a member of the AAUW, Dr Rawson de Dellepiane retained her membership in the NCW after 1910, when most of the AAUW had followed Cecilia Grierson's lead and resigned from that organization. Elvira Rawson was the granddaughter of a North American immigrant; she had grown up in the provincial town of Junín and had been educated at one of Sarmiento's normal schools. Like Cecilia Grierson, she became a physician, but in her case only because the practice of law was closed to women. Despite her declaration that her experiences at the University had destroyed her respect for men, she married Manuel Dellepiane, a Radical politician and lawyer who supported all her activities, and with whom she had seven children.[28]

Dr Rawson de Dellepiane's Feminist Center did not prosper. The NCW had warned her that the word "feminist" would keep people away, and it did. After three months she prudently changed the name to the Manuela Gorritti Center, after a nineteenth century Argentine writer. For thirteen years the Center provided essential community services for women, and a meeting place for feminists.

The Argentine NCW remains today an umbrella organi-

zation for women's associations. Cecilia Grierson is respected by members as an important worker for social
reform and as the founder of the NCW. She is not remembered as a feminist, since the present members of the NCW
do not consider that their organization was ever connected
in any way with feminism. And nothing is known to members of the struggle between Alvina Van Praet de Sala and
Cecilia Grierson.

Notes

[1] *Revista del Consejo Nacional de Mujers*, 1, no 1 (April, 1901), 1.

[2] For a detailed account of the contributing countries and their exhibits see Jeanne Madeline Weimann, *The Fair Woman: The Story of the Woman's Building at the World's Columbian Exposition, Chicago, 1893* (Chgo: Academy Chicago, 1981).

[3] Ernesto Quesada, *La questión femenina* (BA: Pablo E. Coni, 1899), pp. 5-32. Dr Quesada was one of the Generation of Eighty, who worked for intellectualism in Buenos Aires. These people, completely absorbed in European culture, had no confidence that Argentina could develop without foreign influence.

[4] Peter Smith, *Politics and Beef in Argentina: Patterns of Conflict and Change* (NY: Columbia Univ. Press, 1969), p. 17.

[5] Quesada, p. 4.

[6] Cecilia Grierson, "Marcha progresiva de la idea del Consejo Nacional de Mujeres: Trabajo presentado por la Doctora Cecilia Grierson", *Revista del Consejo*, 2, No 8 (1902), 28.

[7] Luis R. Longhi, *Sufragio femenino* (BA: Baiocco, 1932), p. 135. Mrs King had the reputation of being a social climber.

[8] Hernando, "Casa y Familia", p. 190.

[9] Longhi, p. 132.

[10] International Council of Women, *Our Common Cause* (NY: Nat'l Council of Women of the U.S., 1933), pp. 18-24.

[11] Grierson, "Marcha", p. 29.

[12] Moreau, *La mujer en la democracia*, pp. 164-166.

[13] For details of the meeting, see *Revista del Consejo* 1 No 1 (April, 1901), 3-20.

[14] Cecilia Grierson, *Decadencia del Consejo Nacional de Mujeres de la República Argentina* (BA: 1910), pp. 1-5.

[15] *Revista del Consejo 1*, no 4 (15 Dec., 1901), 4.

[16] See Grierson, *Decadencia*, p. 12.

[17] *Revista del Consejo*, p. 32.

[18] *Revista del Consejo 2*, no 2 (25 June, 1902), 4.

[19] *The Evolution of the International Council of Women: Part I, 1888-1913* (NY: NCW of the U.S., 1956), pp. 14-39.

[20] Consejo Nacional de Mujeres de la República Argentina, *Historia de la Biblioteca del Consejo Nacional de Mujeres* (BA: Gráfico "Oceana", 1936), pp. 16-17.

[21] *Revista del Consejo 3*, no 4 (25 Sept., 1903), 38.

[22] *Revista del Consejo 4*, no 4 (5 Sept., 1904), 11.

[23]See International Survey Committee, *International Survey of the Young Men's and Young Women's Christian Associations* (NY: 1932), p. 325; Victor Alberto Mirelman, "The Jews in Argentina, 1890-1930: Assimilation and Particularism" Diss. Columbia Univ., 1973, p. 351. See also Francesco Cordasco and Thomas Monroe Pitkin, *The White Slave Trade and the Immigrants*, (Detroit: Blaine Ethridge, 1981).

[24]*Revista del Consejo 6*, No 6 (25 April, 1907), 18.

[25]Grierson, *Decadencia*, pp. 8-12.

[26]*Historia de la Biblioteca*, p. 23.

[27]Gino Germani, "Mass Immigration and Modernization in Argentina" in *Masses in Latin America*, ed. Irving Louis Horowitz, pp. 289-330.

[28]*El Día*, (Montevideo, N.D.) In Archivo de *La Nación*, B.A.

5

Feminism and the Free Thought Movement
1900-1910

In the last decades of the nineteenth century the circulation of European ideas in Argentina created a belief
that science and evolutionary necessity would cure the
country's deep-seated problems. The upper and middle
classes became convinced that while Latin America lagged
behind Europe and the United States in every aspect of
its development, Argentina and Uruguay, having fewer
Indians and mestizos to retard their progress, were superior to other Latin American nations. These progressives
admired Manuel Belgrano, Bernardino Rivadavia and Domingo Sarmiento, leaders who in the past had attempted
to bring foreign political and economic ideas to Argentina.[1]

The tragedies of the country's history — anarchy, *caudil-
lismo* and civil war — were blamed on Spanish colonialism,
the primitive people in the interior, and the Church.[2] Car-
los Octavio Bunge, whose German-born father was a wealthy
landowner and industrialist, said, "Both [mulattoes and
mestizos] are impure, atavistically anti-Christian; they are
like two heads of a . . . hydra that strangles in its giant coils a
beautiful pale virgin Spanish America."[3]

Although it was considered possible that these primitive
people could be transformed through education and intermarriage, European immigration was a quicker way to improve society, since it was believed that even the poorest,
least educated European could be more easily assimilated

into modern Argentine life than the peon, who relied for his ideas on authority figures.[4]

In 1905, the International Association of Free Thought, which had branches in major European capitals and in several cities in North America, founded the Argentine Association of Free Thought, and made plans to hold its international conference in Buenos Aires in 1910, in order to increase its membership in those Latin American countries which had large European communities.

Argentines who were greatly pleased at this impending honor included members of the landed oligarchy, masons, skilled workers and small businessmen, professional people like doctors, teachers and scientists, non-Catholics and ex-Catholics, and natives and immigrants. As a whole, the free thinkers clustered in the urban centers of Buenos Aires, Rosario, Córdoba and La Plata.[5] In Buenos Aires and La Plata especially, women began to play an important role in AAFT activities. Even before the formal establishment of the organization, women students and normal school teachers had been attracted to the movement; the vast majority of female members were recruited by male relatives, although some women were brought in by unions and mutual aid societies.

Since women were allowed to address the membership of AAFT at a time when public speaking was forbidden to Latin American women, feminist forums were created and between 1900 and 1910 several feminist leaders emerged from the organization, most of whom had been feminists before their free-thinking affiliation but who had not wanted to involve themselves with philanthropic groups like the NCW. Cecilia Grierson and Elvira Rawson de Dellepiane enthusiastically supported the AAFT since it called for full citizenship and equality for women. The AAFT supported Dr Rawson de Dellepiane's Feminist Center and the formation of new women's groups either as AAFT auxiliaries or as separate entities. Auxiliary status provided independence and at the same time allowed women to enjoy the intellectual stimulation of the larger group.[6]

Liberals, socialists, anarchists and other leftists shared with the free thinkers a dedication to "universal rationalism" and anti-clericalism. All of them competed for influence over the AAFT, which opposed the role of religion in marriage; the death penalty; cloistered convents, which they called "an offense to civilization"[7] and "an insult to liberty";[8] and demanded secular co-education, civil marriage, legal divorce and other anti-clerical reforms. In fact, civil registration of marriage had been required by law since 1884 and civil marriage had been legal in Argentina since 1889. Most leaders of the free thinkers were leery of party affiliations: they distrusted the anarchists and were put off by the fact that many Socialists were not anti-clerical. Truth, the AAFT leaders believed, must stem only from scientific observation and the ultimate cure for the world's ills must come from science and mass education based on scientific observation. They were heavily influenced by Herbert Spencer's application of Darwinian evolutionary theory to the study of society. For them sociology, medicine and education were the body of knowledge that would free society from superstition and ignorance. Like the Victorians, the Argentine free thinkers transformed Darwinism into a metaphysics of nature, a prescription for a new life.[9] Spencerian sociology was for them the equivalent of a progressive and optimistic religion.

The free thinkers also shared with the Victorians a belief in the moral superiority of women, which had led the Victorians to give women a strong voice in matters of education, philanthropy and public morality. Women were seen as intuitive and irrational, but possessing delicate sensibilities which, when neglected, caused them to lead fantasy lives. Biological determinism was rejected in popular evolutionism; psychic evolution was held to be both possible and necessary. Thus if men allowed women to evolve properly, the sexes could truly complement each other. Feminine intuition and sensibility would temper male egoism, the primary drive in the struggle for survival, and the use of brute force would be devalued.[10] Women could, if they became more rational without sacrificing their intuitive qualities, cause a "rise in the social emotions" which would replace lust and the urge for domination with "civilized sexuality." The Catholic Latin traditions had stunted women's intellectual development, but individual men were also responsible: male egoism had confined woman to the home, where she was viewed as human property. This imbalance of power distorted the emotional relationships between the sexes.[11]

The prevailing Argentine male values of the late nineteenth and early twentieth centuries were that men should, first, be good providers; that, second, they should pursue unattached females; third, that they should use prostitutes, and finally, that they should deprecate love as a deep emotion.[12] But before anything could be done to change any of this, the free thinkers held that organized religion must be replaced by a belief in science. As early as the 1880s in the normal school system, and particularly in the laboratory at Paraná, student teachers had been taught that Argentine backwardness and the undeveloped personalities of Argentine women were caused largely by the Church's perpetuation of colonial tradition and its rejection of rationalism.

Although the AAFT condemned traditional marriage as legalized prostitution, they did not by any means endorse free love. Women's needs, they felt, were more spiritual than physical — the feminists too believed that women's sexual impulses were weaker than men's — but fulfilling relationships could be found only in monogamous civil marriage. They sponsored sex education meetings, and wished to have sex education — lessons in anatomy and information about pregnancy and venereal disease — taught in the schools by doctors and scientists.[13] Although they considered that procreation was not the only purpose of marital relations, they did not discuss birth control. Eugenics interested them as part of the improvement of future generations and psychology could replace the role of the priest in family life. With the Church gone, men could help the women in their families to achieve a new dignity and self-respect. This idea was popular with Argentine feminists who, building on the traditional Latin image of the idealized mother, believed that motherhood was woman's most important experience. They took from Ellen Key, the Swedish feminist, and from Froebel, the German educator, the idea that the state was obligated, in return for the human resources with which women provided it, to give them legislative protection and welfare benefits. The Argentines continued to elaborate on these ideas for years after they were considered out of date in feminist and educational circles in the United States and Europe.[14]

Josefina Durbec de Routin (1875- ?), a poet and teacher, founded a School for Rational Education, funded by the AAFT, where she taught that arbitrary male power in the home enslaved women both morally and intellectually. María Theresa Ferrari (1887-1956), a medical doctor and pioneer in experimental psychology, also worked with the AAFT; the home, she said, was the greatest experimental laboratory for the situation of women. She was particularly interested in exploring the possibility of psychological factors in women's diseases like hysteria and pregnancy-related illnesses. She had started her own primary school at the age of sixteen.

To those who argued that female morality would be affected by the removal of the constraints of Church and family, the AAFT replied that the new woman would develop an ethical structure through the use of reason to fill the vacuum left by the disappearance of religion. Education would provide an authentic morality, and the ethics of science would determine the future.

Buenos Aires was the cultural center of Latin America. As in Vienna at that time, its cafes were filled with impassioned free thinkers discussing philosophy, literature, science and art with confidence, since intellectual specialization had not yet compartmentalized thought and knowledge.[15] And Argentines made up for their geographical isolation from Europe by frequent travel there and voluminous correspondence. However, respectable women were barred from these cafes at least until the 1920s. Feminists did not attempt to flaunt convention by appearing there, since they believed their lives should be exemplary; they did not want to call down upon themselves the calumny visited in other countries on women who rebelled openly against social structures.[16] In addition, many of these women were temperance workers whose presence in a cafe was unthinkable. However they could participate in evening meetings and discussion groups sponsored by the AAFT and related groups. Because of this acceptance of women in political and intellectual circles, they could meet people outside their families and their work, a situation that was particularly important for writers and artists. For instance, the poet Alfonsina Storni (1892-1938) met writers and publishers whom she could otherwise never have been able to contact, and these friends helped to dispel the feelings of alienation and loneliness to which the solitary writer is prone. Since Alfonsina Storni was an unwed mother, these friendships were doubly important to her. She wrote:

> Everything is so costly to women! Life is so costly! Our exaggerated sensibility, the complicated world that surrounds us, the systematic distrust of the environment, that terrible sad and permanent presence of "the sex" in everything that the woman does for the public. Everything contributes to crush us![17]

Two other feminists whose attitudes developed during their involvement with the free thought movement were María Abela de Ramírez and Julieta Lanteri de Renshaw.

María Abela de Ramírez, who had nine children, was for many years director of a normal school in La Plata; she contributed articles on education and the "science" of motherhood to newspapers and educational journals. In 1902 she founded a feminist monthly journal, *Nosotras*: she believed in the innate superiority of women, who must, however, learn to temper their sensibility with reason to extend their sphere of influence for the good of society. She was an active member of AAFT, agreeing with them about sex education, women's political and civil rights, and the destructive influence of the Church. [18] Despite this her iron will and refusal to compromise made her difficult to work with. She was chosen to chair the National Free Thought Convention in La Plata in 1907, but this honor was withdrawn: Juan Balestra, an AAFT leader, announced that it had been decided that the chairmanship was too great a responsibility for the mother of a large family, and in any case Argentine women were too inexperienced to undertake the organization of a national convention. The meeting place was changed to Córdoba.

The result of this slight was that Señora Ramírez became even more aggressive and combative, alienating the male AAFT members from feminist positions. She began, with Dr Julieta Lanteri, to build a separate National Association of Women Free Thinkers. Dr Lanteri de Renshaw (1873-1932), who had been born in Italy and brought to Argentina by her parents when she was six, had graduated from normal school, received a degree in pharmacology from the National College of La Plata in 1898 and a medical degree from the University of Buenos Aires in 1906, specializing in mental illness and the diseases of women and children.[19] Like other women of her generation she had a difficult time in medical school and was particularly bitter because she was not appointed Professor of Psychiatric Ailments at the Medical School of Buenos Aires, despite having been recommended for the post by two prominent specialists. The reason given was that she did not qualify because she was not an Argentine citizen.[20]

Only one female immigrant had previously applied for citizenship: Mariana Chertkoff de Justo, who, because she was the wife of Juan B. Justo, the founder of the Argentine Socialist party, was granted citizenship without political rights. It was made clear to her at the time that she was granted citizenship only because of her husband. Despite this disheartening precedent, Dr Lanteri too applied for citizenship. It was denied to her because of her sex. Although the Argentine Constitution did not deny women the vote, citizenship was one of the main requirements for suffrage; the government did not want to confront the issue of woman suffrage.[21] Foreign-born women were not granted citizenship unless, like Mariana Chertkoff, they were married to well-known men. In 1910 Dr Lanteri married Dr Albert Renshaw a man of sufficient prominence to cause the government to grant his wife citizenship the following year.

Dr Lanteri, who belonged to the AAUW and the Feminist Center — although not the NCW, since she disliked its philanthropic bent — had spent the years from 1907 to 1920 in Europe, visiting schools, hospitals and asylums. On her return she organized hospital workers to agitate for health-care reform, including a comprehensive welfare plan for poor women and children that would not penalize unwed mothers. In 1911 she founded the League for the Rights of Mothers and Children and presided over the first Child Welfare Conference. Dr Lanteri believed that women's sanity was often threatened by their environment, an opinion shared by Dr Elvira Rawson. The women held that biological differences were being used as an excuse to exclude women from full participation in national life. Like other Argentine feminists, Dr Lanteri believed that women were morally superior to men. In 1906 she had written:

> The female is as good as the man. The functions of
> [her] brain have not been as varied ... but that does not

mean she is inferior. Feminine evolution should not be the same ... as that of men ... As a species, she might be superior. She has a more distinct and superior character ... Feminism is a force. Feminism is an evolution.[22]

Dr Lanteri spoke often before the AAFT membership; she enjoyed giving predominantly male audiences her views, which included heavy emphasis on male materialism and egoism, behind which, she said, lay an uneasy awareness of the moral superiority of women and the consequent fear of their potential power.

Perhaps understandably under these circumstances, AAFT men were not carried away by enthusiasm for women's rights, and spirited debates on the subject were held. Among those fiercely opposed to the feminists was Juan Balestra, the national Deputy who had announced the removal of the international conference to Córdoba, and who had moved, as he grew older, from liberalism to strong conservatism; he was not as a result well-liked by other members of AAFT. Balestra and a few other Deputies insisted on women's innate inferiority to men, presenting elaborate scientific evidence to support their views. Naturally, clashes resulted between these men and Dr Lanteri, Señora Ramírez and Alicia Moreau whose father, Armando, was a prominent Socialist. Bad feeling accelerated to the point where Alicia Moreau demanded that the AAFT choose between her and Balestra. She won the confrontation because Balestra's right-wing politics had alienated most of the membership. In 1910 he joined with vigilantes in attacks on the offices of left-wing newspapers.

Dr Lanteri and Señora Ramírez met with feminists from the Socialist party and the Feminist Center to discuss what they saw as contradictions in the position of the AAFT, who, while they supported most women's issues, were concerned that the Church would exercise its traditional power over women to dictate their vote. This was a major liberal objection to female suffrage in Latin America. In addition, most members of AAFT wished to defer the struggle for woman suffrage until the achievement of universal male suffrage, which was to come in 1912 with the passage of the Sáenz Peña Law. The feminists wanted both goals to be sought at the same time; it was infuriating to them that poor, ignorant men should vote while educated women remained disenfranchised. On the other hand, the women supported the AAFT's stand in favor of legal divorce, but not without trepidation. Although they believed in the principle, they were worried about the effect of divorce on women who had no civil rights and thus no protection against loss of their children and of financial support.

The Free Thinkers used evolution as an argument against religion and for social reform; the feminists likewise attempted to put a scientific base under their demands for full equality. This was not an argument peculiar to Argentines: by the late nineteenth century all feminist arguments, which fifty years earlier had centered upon education, had become anthropological debate about woman's peculiar genius and destiny.[23] And since the significance of sex differences in the higher forms of life was unclear, feminists tended to take up romance where science left off.

They picked up the romantic tradition of Argentine women's literature, in which women poets especially wrote endlessly about the virtues of female martyrs.[24] Julieta Lanteri believed that the exalted "female soul" and the idealized mother were better substitutes for religion than the AAFT's human interaction and family life. Woman was the creative force, doomed to eternal martyrdom unless evolutionary ethics were allowed to guide society, and men were willing to become feminists. One of her speeches gives a typical flavor:

> Man, the master of the earth, made woman his slave and himself her lord. She remained subjugated and with her, her children . . . The arrogant self-interest of

man drove him to make himself the owner of everything, even the innocent goldfinch, which he caged . . .
Master of woman, man made himself master of her
children, her legitimate property, fruit of her womb
. . . flesh of her flesh . . . ! He branded her, he gave her
his name! . . . making her produce the offspring he desired. And when the offspring was female and could
not plow the land, man cursed her birth and destined
her to vulgar reproduction like a cow in a barn . . .

The years have passed . . . And in this present
woman, the luminous light that does not know herself,
continues bound . . . giving him the children he desires, suffering the laws he imposes upon her, eating
the bread that he decides to give her, living where he
wishes her to live . . . she hides her own name and toler-
ates being called the weaker sex. Poor woman! Poor
woman!

Hope begins to shine on the dark horizon. Woman is
awakening to the consciousness of her own worth.
Fires can be seen . . . on South American soil never
reached by the light of the North. Woman raises her
banner with the colors of free thought. She wants
neither to be master nor to recognize masters. For her,
everyone is equal, one race and one species, for she is
the mother of all. For [her], property does not exist,
and she will not kill to preserve it. The whole earth is
her country.[25]

The impassioned, dedicated women resented bitterly
their lack of access to society; they could not move freely
through the streets of cities because it was not considered
proper for women to go out at night without a male escort.
Those who did were subjected to ridicule and harrassment.
In addition, many felt restricted by their clothing; feminists
in most countries talked about "dress reform". Yards of
material and tight corsets were uncomfortable in the hot
summers of the littoral; long sweeping skirts restricted
movement and were unhygienic. Dr Elvira Rawson believed that restrictive clothing combined with lack of exercise to cause a variety of physical and neurotic symptoms in

her middle class female patients.[26] But there was no experimentation with clothing in Argentina. Julieta Lanteri chose to dress in white, lacey garments regardless of the weather; for her, white symbolized the moral purity and spirituality of the female soul.[27] In photographs María Abela de Ramírez is dressed formally, posing with her children like any middle class matron.

The AAFT provided a lively forum for discussion of all reforms by upper and new middle class liberals who "worshipped at the altar of progress and science."[28] Women profited especially since they were able to meet and set up networks for future feminist campaigns. Because of the AAFT, as well as the NCW, the Argentine feminist movement began earlier than similar movements in other Latin American countries. After 1919, however, tension between adherents of various philosophies within the AAFT and their own growing restlessness impelled feminists to turn to the Socialist party to which most of them, along with a large number of male free thinkers, already belonged.

Notes

[1]See Roberto Etchepareborda, "La Estructura Socio-Política Argentina y la Generación del Ochenta", LARR Vol 13 (1978), 127-134; Thomas McGann, *Argentina, the United States and the International System. 1880-1914* (Cambridge, Mass: Harvard Univ. Press, 1957); Sandra McGee, "The Social Origins of Counterrevolution in Argentina, 1900-1932" Diss., Univ of Florida, 1979; Alejandro Korn, *Influencias filosóficas en la evolución nacional* (B.A.: Claridad, n.d.); Romero, *A History of Argentine Political Thought*; Leopold Zea, *The Latin American Mind*, transl. by J. Abbot and L. Dunham (Norman, Okla: Univ of Oklahoma Press, 1966), Chapter 8; Juan Adolfo Vázquez, "La filosofía en las Universidades Argentinas" in *Antología filosófica Argentina del siglo XX* (B.A.: Univ of Buenos Aires, 1965), pp. 22-29. See also Scobie, p. 219 for a discussion of upper class attitudes toward native and immigrant labor.

[2]Villarroel, "El génesis de los creencias humanas", p. 49.

[3]Morner, *Race Mixture*, p. 140.

[4]José Luís de Imaz, *Los Que Mandan*, trans. C.A. Astiz (Albany: SUNY Press, 1970), pp. 1-2.

[5]Information specifically about the Argentine Free Thinkers comes from *Album biográfico de los Librepensadores de la República Argentina* (BA: Otto Rossaly, 1910).

[6]Author's interview with Alicia Moreau de Justo, 22 July, 1977.

[7]*Album*, p. 100.

[8]*Ibid*, p. 137, p. 166.

[9]See Teggart and Maurice Mandelbaum, *History, Man and Reason: A Study in Nineteenth Century Thought* (Baltimore: Johns Hopkins Univ Press, 1971), Chaps. 5 and 6, and Jill Conway, "Stereotypes of Femininity", pp. 140-154.

[10]*Album*, p. 184, p. 195.

[11]Men who argued for women's rights in the AAFT meetings were Dr. Caruci, Suárez Corvo, Francisco Gicca and Eusebio Valls. Apart from Alicia Moreau, female feminists were María Abela de Ramírez and Julieta Lanteri, Elisa Picchio and Dorotea de Ros George. Speeches in the *Album* are unsigned.

[12]Scobie, p. 229.

[13]*Album*, pp. 117-118.

[14]*Unión y Labor*, 1909-1913.

[15]See Allan Janik and Stephen Toulmin, *Wittgenstein's Vienna* (NY: Simon & Schuster, 1973), p. 18.

[16]Roberto Guisti, "Alfonsina", *Nosotros* 3, No. 32 (1938), 372-397; Rachel Philips, *Alfonsina Storni: From Poetess to Poet* (London: Tamesis Bks Ltd, 1975), p. 10.

[17]Percas, "Women Poets", p. 42.

[18]*Album*, p. 167.

[19]Julieta Lanteri, *Contribución al estudio del deciduoma maligno* (B.A.: Nicolás Marona, 1906).

[20]William B. Parker, *Argentines of Today* (B.A.: Hispanic Society of America, 1920), p. 41.

[21] Austin F. MacDonald, *Government of the Argentine Republic* (NY: Thomas Crowell, 1942), pp. 117-118.

[22]Julieta Lanteri, "El feminismo es una fuerza" in *Album*, pp. 209-210.

[23]Stites, *Women's Liberation Movement in Russia*", p. 30.

[24]See Percas, "Women Poets", p. 42.

[25]Hollander, pp 152-153.

[26]*Ibid*, p. 190.

[27]"La candidata en la intimidad", *El Hogar* (19 Dec., 1924), p. 6; *Caras y Caretas* (31 Jan, 1920) in *Archivo de la Nación*.

[28]Scobie, p. 109.

6

Feminism and Socialism

In the last decades of the nineteenth century heavy immigration into Argentina immeasureably strengthened the political left: Socialists, syndicalists and anarchists sought refuge in both Argentina and Uruguay from the conservative reaction in Europe to the revolutions of 1848 and the collapse of the Paris commune in 1871; in addition, many immigrants from Southern Europe had in their own countries belonged to trade unions or social reformist groups.[1] This potential for change was galvanized by a serious economic depression in Argentina in 1890, followed by uprisings in the provinces. Progressive members of the Argentine upper class, aware of the movement toward popular democracy in Europe, saw their own cities growing and new social classes gaining strength, and became convinced that it was time to develop truly representative Argentine political parties which could forestall wide-spread unrest by responding quickly to public opinion.

After 1900 these progressives began to move to the new Radical party (*Unión Cívica Radical*) which had been responsible for provincial disruption after its formation in 1892. Although the Radicals were openly dedicated to rebellion to create popular democracy, they did not constitute a political party with a set list of priorities, so much as a kind of vague movement for the social good. Because of this they did not attract the working classes, which gravitated to the left: to the Socialists, syndicalists and anarchists. But in

1895 an unexpectedly strong Radical uprising politicized elements of the public which had been relatively apathetic politically, even though this uprising was weaker than the provincial Radical uprisings of 1893. The government put down the 1895 rebellion without much trouble, but it was sufficiently shaken to declare an amnesty for the rebels in 1906. After that the Radicals gained new energy and much popular support among the urban middle classes; they tightened their party organization and developed a program with strong demands for social reform. They were not interested in women's issues.

At about the same time the anarchists began to establish a presence among the working classes. Anarchism had first appeared in Argentina in the 1880s, among Italian and Spanish immigrants; after 1899, when an economic crisis combined with increased immigration to cause a drop in wages and a rise in rents, the anarchists began to organize trade unions. In 1904 they founded FORA (*Federación Obrera Regional Argentina*), which was the most influential of the anarchist groups, although its twenty thousand members constituted only about five percent of the working class. On several occasions the anarchists, who believed in direct action rather than in bargaining, were able to transform trade disputes into general strikes with huge popular support and uproar in the streets. Because of the dedication of the anarchists, their intransigence against the desires of the oligarchy and their educational programs for workers, including women, which raised Argentina's literacy rate, the period from 1900 to 1910 has been called the "heroic" period of Argentine trade unionism.[2] Although the country's primary business was grain and cattle export, the anarchists had their greatest success organizing workers in light manufacturing and a variety of growing service industries.

From 1895 to 1915 anarchists contributed to the exchange of ideas in both Argentina and Uruguay by running free schools which offered education outside the influence of the state educational system and the Church. They held conferences, organized discussion groups and published newspapers, *La Protesta, La Agitación, El Perseguido* and *Germinal,* which were translated into English and Italian for circulation abroad. European anarchists came to lecture in Argentina. But despite all this intellectual ferment, the anarchists were not really interested in theoretical discussion: they were primarily activists who wanted to destroy the existing social order, to remove the populace from the influence of state and capitalist and Church authority. It was the hierarchical structure of the Church to which they objected rather than religion itself.

Most active feminists had some political connections with groups that agitated for better conditions for workers including women and children, although women constituted only about ten percent of the non-agricultural work force.[3] Most feminists were attracted to the Socialist party, but some interesting women attached themselves to the anarchists, despite the fact that anarchist philosophy was basically hostile to reformist feminist objectives. Argentine anarchists, like those in Southern Europe, romanticised the role of women: to them the idea of woman as emotional support to the alienated male worker was primary. The role of man as protector of the family was, they believed, being eroded by capitalist exploitation of women, and the Church was to blame too, but the Church could not be held responsible for the fact that the head of the family did not receive a wage on which he could support his family without the economic support of his wife. Therefore there was little direct criticism of the Church in anarchist newspapers, although anarchist anti-clerical campaigns received a warm response.[4] Anarchists held that the employment of women distorted the natural sexual division of labor and prevented men from earning a living wage. This idea was of course shared by many women who were not anarchists.[5] Working women, it was believed by anarchists, could not adequately perform their natural roles of wives and mothers and could easily become morally corrupt.

Certainly working conditions for women were not ideal. James Scobie has described them:

> In order to supplement family income, women and children often worked as long hours as men, frequently in cramped, unhealthy surroundings. Most children in [Buenos Aires] attended the first grades of elementary school, but those from the poorer families went to work at the age of nine or ten. Producers of cigarettes, matches, hats, buttons and burlap bags invariably turned to cheap labor — women and children. These shops, which employed anywhere from a dozen to several hundred workers, also saved on light, ventilation and space. Rarely did women and children effectively protest such economies. In addition, piecework from garment stores, as well as the city's laundering and ironing, afforded thousands of women employment at home, the crowded patios and rooms of conventillos and apartment houses.[6]

Working women themselves occasionally attempted to do something about the conditions in which they found themselves. All nineteen founders of the first anarchist Women's Center in Buenos Aires had been unskilled laborers at some time in their lives.

One of the few available sources of primary information about the role of women in the trade unions is a report written for the government in 1904 by Juan Bialet Massé after three years spent touring the provinces. Bialet Massé says that women had an important part in the foundation in 1870 of Córdoba's oldest workers' society, Unión y Progreso, and in the maintainance of the society's activities, which included free education for children and the best workers' library in Argentina, until 1894 when for reasons unknown to Massé, the society prohibited full membership for women and relegated them to auxiliary membership only.[7]

Catholics and conservatives too were interested in

improving working conditions for women. In 1898 four hundred working women in Avellaneda, a working-class area of Buenos Aires, belonged to the Women's Catholic Benevolent Society: opposed to liberalism and all leftist doctrines, and dedicated to the solution of problems through social Catholicism, this group built a workers' hospital in Avellaneda. And Carolina Muzzilli (1880- ?), a consumptive worker who attended Socialist-sponsored education programs, provided reports on the conditions for females working in factories that were used in 1906 in the campaign for protective legislation.

Socialist and liberal reformers, including feminists, did not necessarily advocate the employment of women, but they saw such employment as inevitable and worked therefore to mitigate the unpleasant aspects of it. The anarchists, despite their strong preference for an idealized family to one in which all adult members made financial contributions, felt constrained to support reformers in their humanitarian campaigns to regulate and reform factory work for women and children.[8] In 1907 the anarchists co-operated with feminists and the Socialist Deputy Alfredo Palacios to work for the passage of national laws regulating women's working hours and conditions, for which Carolina Muzzilli had provided information. These laws were passed, but never implemented. In 1898 the anarchists founded the Union of Female Labor to unite workers in predominantly female industries.

In the anarchist ranks were several dozen impressively active women who published books, circulated anarchist literature, organized and participated in strikes and led discussion groups encouraging women not only to fight for better conditions in the workplace, but to widen their horizons after work. Educated women taught at anarchist free schools while they worked during the day to organize women in factories. Thus they recruited new members, encouraging women to participate in anarchist-organized community activities. Immigrant women with left leanings who had given up the Church were able to fill the gap in their lives with anarchist women's groups which operated to a large degree independently of male influence.

Pietro Gori, an Italian anarchist who lectured on penal reform in the School of Criminology at the University of Buenos Aires, was one man who helped to bring women into anarchist circles. He emphasized to male anarchists the importance of increased female membership to the growth of the movement. Gori was basically a reformer, despite his anarchism: he argued at the University for improvement of facilities for male and female prisoners and for research into the causes of criminal behavior. His influence at the School of Criminology was pervasive; already in 1898 it had become a center for advanced thought. Gori's audiences included physicians and sociologists who were interested in rehabilitation rather than punishment and in the social roots of crime and mental illness.[9] Gori estimated that mental disease was probably responsible for the incarceration of fifty percent of Argentina's criminal population.

At the University, Gori recruited women students, stressing not only trade union activity, but the necessity of broadening anarchist activity by working for social reform and ending the exploitation of women in the home as well as the factory. Women found Pietro Gori inspiring. One, who was present at the Progress Club in Buenos Aires when he spoke in May, 1899, recalled the sympathy with which he mentioned the "double slavery" of women at home and at work: "Women! We call upon you to fight together for the abolition of all miseries. We want to abolish contract marriage, which opposes the free union of affection; purify the union of the sexes — introduce the family of love in place of the conventional one."[10]

Gori, who never married, was convinced that legal marriage was inimical to love. But with the exception of Gonzalez Pacheco, an anarchist playwright who proselytized for the individualist doctrines of sexual freedom and human autonomy, Argentine anarchists were not interested in discussion of alternatives to marriage:[11] although they talked about the "lies of legal marriage", they felt that free love, like suffrage and civil rights, were issues for salon feminists or middle-class intellectuals like Pacheco. Many of these working-class radicals had a strong puritanical streak and deplored what they considered to be moral laxity.[12]

In addition to recruiting female students, Gori encouraged women students who had already committed themselves to the anarchist cause before they came to Buenos Aires. One of these was the Uruguayan activist Virginia Bolten, who had helped to organize a successful strike of seamstresses in Rosario in 1889; the women won a twenty percent raise in salary. Gori introduced Virginia Bolten to anarchist intellectual circles in Buenos Aires and helped her to found the first women's anarchist newspaper, *Women's Voice*.

The government was, as might be expected, not happy with all this anarchist and radical activity. It struck back in 1902 and 1910 respectively, with the Law of Residence and the Law of Social Defense, making deportation or imprisonment the punishment for engaging in anarchist activities. Consequently Virginia Bolten was deported several times to Uruguay. In 1903 she was arrested for distributing anarchist literature in Rosario. In 1904 she organized the women's strike committee at the fruit market in Buenos Aires. Her comrade Juana Rouco Buela was deported to Spain because of her participation in a tenant strike in 1907 when she was eighteen years old. She returned to Argentina in 1910.

Both Virginia Bolten and Juana Rouco Buela belonged to various labor federations in Rosario and Buenos Aires. Like Emma Goldman and Voltairine Le Clayre in the United States, they were travelling anarchist organizers, persuasive public speakers well-known for their advocacy of female militancy in politics.[13] They, and others like them, were not interested in universal suffrage, as the Socialist women were. To them feminism was palliative. They did not want to tinker with the status quo; they wanted to destroy it completely. Some anarchist women were active also in the AAFT and the Uruguayan Rationalist League, founded in Montevideo in 1902; they moved freely between Buenos Aires and Montevideo; some had homes in both cities. But there was only spasmodic collaboration between the Free Thinkers and the anarchists; there was no consistent cooperation.

Although women participated in the anarchist movement in Argentina from 1885 to 1910, there were few notable women leaders, with the exception of Virginia Bolten and Juana Rouco Buela. And little is known about them. It is known that Virginia Bolten founded, with Pietro Gori, an organization of socialists and anarchists dedicated to the dissolution of conventional marriage and other authoritarian concepts, and that she lived openly for years with her lover, the anarchist Manrique.[14] Juana Rouco Buela wrote her autobiography, *Historia de un ideal vivido por una mujer* (*History of an Ideal Lived by a Woman*); she was the daughter of working-class Spanish immigrants and was brought into the movement by her brother, Ciriaco, an organizer in Buenos Aires. On the whole, anarchist women seem to have been impressive. Alicia Moreau de Justo has said that Socialist women were awed by their ideological sophistication and their courage, although the Socialists disliked anarchism and the clandestine nature of its activities.[15] In general, working-class women did not respond any more favorably to anarchism than educated Socialist women, despite the fact that anarchists did not espouse causes like divorce and free love which threatened the mass of women, who did not want men to be freed from their familial responsibilities. And anarchist women were doubtless somewhat overpowering. Juana Rouca Buela said with some contempt that women lacked courage; they were too frightened and conservative to fight.[16]

Most bourgeois feminists were thus more comfortable in the Socialist party, apart from the fact that the government policy of repression, which culminated in 1910 with vigilante attacks on anarchist printing presses and meeting halls, and in official banishments and prison terms, destroyed the effectiveness of the anarchists. The Socialists who fought the anarchists for the allegiance of the Argentine working classes were basically moderates. They stood for liberal reform, the parliamentarian concept, popular democracy, separation of church and state, and free trade, and they were the first political party to come out for woman suffrage. In addition they wanted legal divorce and the abolition of legalized prostitution and the white slave trade. In the area of reform, they wanted an eight-hour workday and the expansion of primary education.[17]

The Socialist party was founded in 1894 by Juan B. Justo (1865-1928), a medical doctor who led the party until his death. It was tightly knit, with consistent objectives, and its members came mainly from the professional and small manufacturing classes rather than from the working class. Radicalism its members rejected as old-fashioned and disorganized, and anarchism because of its negativism and violence. Because the trade unions in their turn rejected Socialism, the Socialists worked to qualify immigrants for suffrage—no easy task, since most immigrants did not want to give up their original citizenship. Before 1912, when universal manhood suffrage broadened their base somewhat, the Socialists had only one electoral success, the election of Alfredo Palacios to Congress from the Boca district of Buenos Aires.[18]

Women were admitted to full membership in the party, but the few women who were active were related to male Socialists; these women were encouraged in the first decades of the twentieth century to found Socialist Women's

Centers. A small number of the organizers of the Socialist Women's Center in La Boca, which helped to organize female weavers and seamstresses were working-class immigrants. One such was Carolina Muzzilli, who, because of her diligence, her experience as a factory worker and a recommendation from the Beneficent Society, was recommended by the province of Buenos Aires to study women's working conditions in the cigar and textile industries. Her report, published in *La Prensa*, described long hours, inadequate machinery, dangerous and unhealthy conditions and physical and sexual abuse of women workers. She became a public figure overnight, and to Catholic reformers like Celia La Palma de Emery presented an example of the potential in working-class women, even though Carolina Muzzilli became a Socialist.[19]

Two other women who helped with the Socialist Centers were Gabriela de Laperrière de Coni and Fenia Chertkoff de Repetto. Gabriela de Coni (1866-1906), a French immigrant, was the first woman to serve on the Socialist party executive committee. In 1899 she had married Dr Emilio de Coni, a prominent Socialist thirty years her senior; it was doubtless he who brought her into the party. She was an attractive woman who, in addition to political work and public speaking, wrote naturalistic novels widely read in Argentina although they were never translated from their original French. She was a lover of luxuries, much criticized by the somewhat puritanical Socialists, including her husband, for her extravagances. In 1904 she caused a considerable scandal when she left the party to marry her lover, Julio Arraga, her husband's best friend and a syndicalist, who were more popular among the workers than the Socialists. As would be expected, Gabriela de Coni then promptly joined the syndicalist movement. Since her behavior outraged liberals who believed in monogamy and the simple life, she has received scant attention in histories of early Argentine feminism. In 1901 she organized a national peace conference and the following year founded a workers' pacifist league. She died of tuberculosis at an early age.[20]

Fenia Chertkoff (1869-1928) came from an actively socialist Russian immigrant family. Her father, Moises Chertkoff, constantly plagued by the Tsarist police in the family's native Odessa, emigrated to Argentina in 1904. Her sisters Mariana and Adela were both married to prominent Argentine Socialists: Mariana was the first wife of Juan B. Justo and Adela was married to Adolfo Dickman, a party leader and theoretician and the brother of Enrique Dickman. Mariana was not politically active and died young. But Fenia and Adela worked with Socialist and Feminist Women's Centers.

Fenia had emigrated to Argentina from Odessa in 1895, a widow with a small child. Her husband had been Gabriel Gucovsky, a prominent Russian Socialist. She settled in the province of Entre Ríos, in the Santa Clara Colony, an agricultural settlement founded by Eastern European Jews with the financial backing of Baron Maurice Hirsch, a well-known philanthropist. Fenia, who had graduated from normal school in Odessa, founded a library and a primary school in Santa Clara. In 1897 and 1898 she travelled to Europe to visit her sister-in-law Victoria Gucovsky, who lived in Switzerland, having been exiled from Russia because of her political activities, and who was later to emigrate to Argentina, settle in Santa Clara and marry another Socialist, Antonio de Tomaso. In Europe Fenia learned about Froebelian educational techniques and about the international feminist movement. Upon her return she moved to Buenos Aires and joined the party. In 1910 she too married a Socialist, Nicolas Repetto, a founding member. In addition to her political activities Fenia Chertkoff was an accomplished sculptor. Unfortunately she was bedridden for the last twenty years of her life but, like Florence Nightingale in similar circumstances, she issued a stream of tracts on politics, feminism and child development.

Obviously the sharing of political commitments by male and female Socialists led in many cases to a sharing of lives. The women found that romantic relationships within the party helped them to bear illness, poverty and inevitable political disillusionments and disappointments.[21]

Two impressive women were related to Juan B. Justo: one was his sister Sara and the other was his second wife, Alicia Moreau. In addition to being among the first group of practicing female dentists in Argentina, Sara Justo (1870-1941) was one of the founders of the AAUW, of the Socialist Feminist Center and the Socialist Women's Centers. She taught courses in domestic science and was the director of two commercial schools for women. She held to the position that women were morally superior to men and that motherhood provided a strong impulse for reform. In 1909 she went to Europe to study women's movements there; she was particularly impressed by the Italian movement — even the NCW in Italy, she said, was more serious and open-minded than its Argentine counterpart. The English feminists she found too radical; she was repelled by what she called their "exhibitionism".

She returned home eager to inform the Argentine women's movement about her European experiences. She felt that these were germane since a large part of the Argentine population was Italian and, like the Argentines, the Italians were Catholic and conservative by nature. She believed that what was needed was a feeling of unity among women and a breaking of class boundaries. In addition, the Italians had encouraged her to lead the temperance fight in Argentina, because alcohol clearly caused women much misery.

But now the NCW, the professional women and the Socialists were almost totally at odds with one another. In addition, the Argentine NCW refused to be identified in any way with even the most superficial reforms advocated by European NCWs. Despite the fact that she wrote a book about her European observations (*Movemiento femenino en Europa* or *The Women's Movement in Europe*) and lectured, few women outside the Socialist Party were interested in Sara Justo's enthusiastic idealism.[22] On Socialist women she did have influence. She worked with them to prepare women for the eventual responsibility of citizenship. Educated women could not, she believed, be refused suffrage; she was willing to accept qualified suffrage for the educated woman, a position with which most Socialists could not agree.[23]

When Mariana Chertkoff, Juan B. Justo's first wife, died, Sara and her mother took over the responsibilites of Juan's home and children for eight years until in 1922 Juan married Alicia Moreau. Sara did not view this marriage with equanimity, with the consequence that two of the most important Argentine feminist leaders remained personal enemies throughout Sara's life.[24]

Alicia Moreau was born of French parents in 1885 in England, where her father, Armando, was living in exile because of his activities in the Paris Commune of 1870. When Alicia was a small child Armando emigrated with his family to Argentina where he worked as an influential journalist and Socialist leader. Alicia accompanied her father to meetings and demonstrations in Buenos Aires and at the age of fifteen helped her friends Fenia Chertkoff and Gabriela de Coni to found the Socialist Feminist Center; she taught child care there and at the Socialist Women's Center in the working class Buenos Aires district of La Boca. She, like Julieta Lanteri, Elvira Rawson and Cecilia Grierson, studied medicine at the University of Buenos Aires and encountered great hostility from male students, although the faculty, she says, was supportive. She attributes part of the male student's hostility to her own personal beauty; they were offended, she says, because she did not want to marry any of them, and consequently she was more persecuted than less attractive women. At the same time she says that the male students were angry because they knew that women were naturally better doctors than men.

Even before she began her studies at the University, Alicia Moreau was a respected social worker and writer. Her articles appeared in the Socialist daily newspaper *La Vanguardia*, in her father's journal *The New Humanity* (*La Nueva Humanidad*) and her collaborations with other Socialists and feminists on educational and psychological themes were published by the party publishing house, Ateneo Popular. In 1911 she wrote a short book, *Feminism in Social Evolution* (*El feminsimo en la evolutión social*), discussing the connection of socialism and feminism with historical human evolution. The "scientific" necessity for feminism Dr. Moreau learned, she said, as a result of her University training: industrialism had made feminism a necessity; women were entitled to the fruits of their own labor. While it was true that educated mothers could wean their sons from violence and alcohol, the maternal role did not justify exclusion of women from the public sphere. On the contrary, the importance of women in the home, along with their new economic roles outside the home, was justification for the granting of women's political and civil rights.

Her belief in the necessity of women's employment was one reason for Alicia Moreau's rejection of anarchism; their propensity for violence was another. She worked with the AAFT and in 1906 she was elected to the AAFT board. She attended meetings with her friend Isolina Sáenz de Centeno, a writer and an aristocratic member of the NCW, one of the few female members of the oligarchy with whom Dr Moreau was friendly. With feminist doctors like Julieta Lanteri and Elvira Rawson she got on fairly well, but she disapproved of the individualism of the feminists; they did not, in her opinion, put sufficient emphasis on the larger struggle for social justice. She had been raised as a Socialist and remained one to her dying day, although her belief in evolutionary necessity had waned.

In her book, *The Civil Emancipation of Women* (1919), Alicia Moreau attacked the "Argentine-Hispano Criolle mentality" which promoted what she called "the child-doll personality" and which, while allowing eighty-seven percent of Argentine primary school teachers to be women, denied these same women civil and political equality. European immigrant women, she said, were more free both psychologically and socially than native Argentines, and it was their mission to educate and liberate the native population.[25]

Notes

[1] Between 1859 and 1932, approximately five million people emigrated to Argentina from Europe. See Germani, "Mass Immigration and Modernization", p. 292.

[2] See Victor Alba, *Politics and the Labor Movement in Latin America* (Stanford: Stanford Univ. Press, 1968); Robert Alexander, *Organized Labor in Latin America* (NY: Free Press, 1965); Sebastián Marotta, *El movimiento sindical Argentino: su génesis y desarollo, 1857-1914* (BA: Ediciones Libera, 1960); Scobie, *Buenos Aires*, pp. 235-249; Hobart Spalding, *La clase trabajadora Argentina: documentos para su historia, 1890-1912* (BA: Editorial Galerna, 1970); Mark Szuchman, *Mobility and Integration in Urban Argentina: Córdoba in the Liberal Era* (Austin: Univ. of Texas, 1980), p. 5.

[3] Some work has been done on Argentine women's labor. See Donna Guy, "Women, Peonage and Industrialization: Argentina, 1810-1914" in *LARR* Vol. 16 no 3 (1981), 81; Hollander, "Women in the Political Economy of Argentina"; Zulma R. de Lattés and Catalina Wainerman, "Empleo femenino y desarrollo económico" in *Desarrollo Económico 17*, no 66, (July-Sept. 1977), 301-317; Judith Lynn Sweeney, "Immigrant Women in Argentina, 1890-1914" Thesis, Univ. of Cal., 1977.

[4] See Temma Kaplan, "Female Consciousness and Collective Action: The Case of Barcelona, 1910-1918,": *Signs* vol. 7, No. 3 (Spring, 1982): 545-546.

[5] Spalding, *La clase trabajadora*, p. 141.

[6] Scobie, 143.

[7] Juan Bialet Massé, *El estado de las clases obreras Argentinas a comienzos del siglo*, (Córdoba: Universidad Nacional de Córdoba, 1968), p. 443.

[8] Information on Argentine anarchism comes from Richard A. Yoast, "The Development of Argentine Anarchism: A Socio-Ideological Analysis" Diss. Univ. of Wis., 1975. See also James Joll, *The Anarchists* (Boston: Little Brown, 1964) p. 175.

[9] Jorge Larroca, "Un anarchista en Buenos Aires" in *Todo es Historia*. no 47 (March, 1971), 45-57.

[10] *Ibid*, p. 52.

[11] Yoast, p. 355.

[12] Juana Rouco Buela, *Historia de un ideal vivido por una mujer* (BA: Julio Kaufman, 1964). Besides Virginia Bolten, active female anarchists listed here were María Collazo, Teresa Capporaletti, Violeta García, Elisa Leotar, Marta Newelstein and María Reyes.

[13] See Paul Avrich, *An American Anarchist: The Life of Voltairine Le Cleyre* (Princeton: Princeton Univ. Press, 1978). Alix Kates Shulman, *Red Emma Speaks: Selected Writings and Speeches by Emma Goldman* (NY: Vintage, 1972).

[14] Rouco Buela, p. 27.

[15] Emilio Corbiére, "Alicia Moreau de Justo" Revista LYRA, Vol. 231, no. 2 (1977).

[16] Rouco Buela, p. 74.

[17] José Ratzer, *Los Marxistas Argentinos del 90* (Córdoba: Ediciones Pasado y Presente, 1969), p. 16.

[18] Peter Smith, *The Politics of Beef in Argentina: Patterns of Conflict and Change* (NY: Columbia, 1969), pp. 22-26. For information on Juan B. Justo, see Alicia Moreau de Justo, *El Socialismo de Juan B. Justo* (BA: Editorial Polis, 1946); Juan B. Justo, *Socialismo* (B.A.: La Vanguardia, 1920): Jacinto Oddone, *Declaración de principios y programa del partido socialista* (BA: Partido Socialista Democrática, 1972); Donald Weinstein, "Juan B. Justo: An Argentine Socialist" Diss. CUNY, 1974.

[19] Sweeney, "Immigrant Women in Argentina", p. 41.

[20] For information on Gabriela de Coni see Enrique Dickman, *Recuerdos de un militante socialista* (BA: La Vanguardia, 1949); Antonio Pages Larraya, *Gabriela de Coni y su precursoras* (BA: Edicíones Culturales, 1965).

[21] Dickman, *Recuerdos*, pp. 42-45, 202.

[22] Sara Justo, *Movimiento femenino en Europa* (BA: Gráfico Collins, 1909).

[23] *Caras y Caretas*, Vol. 32, no. 1625 (23 Nov., 1929).

[24] Author's interview with Alicia Moreau de Justo, 22 July, 1977.

[25] Alicia Moreau de Justo, *La emancipación civil de la mujer* (BA: Unión Feminista Nacional, 1919), pp. 1-2. See also Moreau de Justo, *El feminismo en la evolución social* (BA: Ateneo Popular, 1911), p. 3.

7

The International
Feminist Congress of 1910

I have known in Buenos Aires some forty female doctors who practice medicine, surgery, dentistry, anthro-
pology and obstetrics. I visited a class at the Academy
of Medicine which was directed by a woman. I also visited a school of massage and of nursing founded and
directed by a woman; and on more than one occasion
listened to speeches given publicly by acclaimed and
renowned women . . . In the various salons where I was
received, women performed music which they themselves had composed . . . one woman wore the medal of
heroes, earned for her aid in a field hospital during a
battle. I read stories, poetry, books and school texts,
novels, newspaper articles, scientific tracts, medical
manuals, all published by women. I admired, in the
Parliament of Buenos Aires, statues and bas reliefs
chiselled by a sculptress; I learned that the administration of all hospitals and of all charity works in the
Argentine Republic are in the hands of women.

Travel Diary of Gina Lombroso Ferrero, 1907[1]

The year 1910 was an important one for Argentina; it was
the hundreth year of independence. And it was an important year for the Argentine women's movement; two major
women's conferences were held, representing the gamut of
female political thought. The conservative position was
given at the conference sponsored by the government-
funded National Council of Women in April and the left-
wing or feminist position at the First International Feminist Congress of Argentina held two months earlier on

February twentieth and organized chiefly by the Argentine Association of University Women.

The NCW Conference opened on April nineteenth; the inaugural address was given by Alvina Van Praet de Sala, the President of both the NCW and the Beneficent Society. Attending dignitaries included leading clergy and Roque Sáenz Peña, the President of the Republic. Most of the participants and guests were related to the women who had helped in the struggle for national independence one hundred years earlier, and not unexpectedly emphasis was put on the historical continuity between the actions of the national heroines of the past and the philanthropic activities of modern Argentine women. Patriotism was the note of the hour: nationalist poetry was read, and the work of the Catholic women's charities was extolled. Although the tone of the conference was thus largely positive and self-congratulatory, a touch of defensiveness could be noted in some of the speeches. President Van Praet de Sala herself said specifically in her opening remarks: "The culture for women which our institution pursues is not in any manner commonly understood as feminism."[2] This statement was later made the theme of a literary contest, sponsored by the NCW, for female public and parochial school students.

A speech by Celia La Palma de Emery appeared to reflect the reaction of philanthropic and pious women to the Feminist Congress which had been held two months earlier. Her subject, the necessity of counteracting the influence of left-wing ideology on working-class women, was a familiar one to her audience.[3] She had addressed the problem before various Catholic philanthropic organizations and religious congresses; in 1908 she had lectured in Uruguay as well as in Argentina. The women of the NCW should, she said, counteract leftist influence by working for the implementation of protective legislation, and by recruiting women into the Circle of Catholic Workers through working-girls' clubs and visits to their homes:

> Our action at the present [she said] in order to win
> the hearts of the woman worker, has to be limited to
> the times when she is weak, over-worked or sick, and
> . . . needs some means of subsistence, provided by the
> delicate care of charity . . . [Her] relatives will see our
> abnegation, will be grateful for it, and will therefore
> surrender themselves before the love of God. In this
> way, how many times will we not succeed in winning
> over an entire family?[4]

Even this sort of delicate lobbying may have been too close to direct action to suit many NCW members. The sense of the meetings was that women should influence society only through their children, whom they should educate to act for the civic good.[5] The firmness of this stand was undoubtedly a reaction to increased demand for suffrage from feminists. Alvina Van Praet de Sala believed firmly that the overwhelming majority of Argentine women of all classes shared the values of the NCW. And indeed the conference itself flowed smoothly, with no dissent and much pleasant social activity.

The feminist conference was officially titled the First International Feminist Congress of Argentina (*Primer Congreso Femenino Internacional de la República Argentina* or FIFC). The organizers of the Congress used the word "international" in order to lend scope and dignity to their meeting; prominent foreign feminists were made honorary sponsors to lend legitimacy to the enterprise: these included Marie Curie, Ellen Key of Sweden and Maria Montessori who, although not physically present, had sent papers to be read aloud.[6] Because of their strong cultural identification with Europe, Argentine feminists had looked there for models, even though the center of feminist activity for the past three decades had been the United States. Thus unfortunately the Argentines were isolated from important North American trends of thought until the 1920s.

Fenia Chertkoff was quoted by the Argentine press as saying that the FIFC represented the first South American movement of women against male reactionaries; "real" Argentine women who cared about their homes and families would attend the FIFC, she said, rather than the NCW Conference; women now wanted their full rights as Argentine citizens.[7]

The Congress was opened on 20 February at the Italian Opera Center in Buenos Aires by Petrona Eyle, the President, who duly thanked the Congress planners (Sara Justo, Julieta Lanteri, Elvira Rawson de Dellepiane, Cecilia Grierson, Ernestina López and Fenia Chertkoff) and the Argentine shipping and railway companies which had discounted fares for participants who had come from the interior and from Chile and Uruguay; and welcomed these participants and those who had come from Peru, Italy and the United States. Several Italian feminists had come to Buenos Aires to help set up the Children's House, which would be comprised of an orphanage, a primary school and a home for unwed mothers, modeled on an Italian institution directed by Maria Montessori.

For the purposes of the FIFC, feminism was defined as "the evolution of women toward superior ideals and woman's participation in the progress of humanity."[8] This loose definition left definite goals open to discussion and vote by the attending membership of four hundred women.

The inaugural address was given by Ernestina López (1879-1965) who, in 1903, had been the first woman to earn a doctorate in Arts and Letters from the University of Buenos Aires. Her speech, which was intended to place the Argentine woman's movement in historical perspective, lasted over an hour and contained considerable exaggeration of the progress made by North American and European women; this exaggeration was typical of Argentine feminist speeches of the period and was probably meant to shame Argentines into competition and to encourage the belief that what had been possible in other countries was possible also in Argentina. Dr. López heaped praise on the "progressive" men of North America; Argentine men were more difficult, she said, but they could be won over just as European and North American men had been. She called upon the ladies of the Beneficent Society and the NCW to join with Argentine professional women in working for the improvement of society; the FIFC sessions on education and social work would prove to the conservative philan- thropists that feminists did not desire to destroy the family — quite the contrary.

The remainder of the address was devoted to a defense of women's behavior in the light of their position in Argentine society; an attack on the refusal of men to accept women in the workplace and on female artists who remained selfishly apolitical and basically anti-social, along with a refutation of an oft-repeated argument that women's brains were small- er than men's. Dr López concluded by saying that the lack of participation by women in the issues of the twentieth cen- tury could mean the downfall of civilization.[9]

The first few days of the FIFC were taken up with sub- committee sessions. The Congress was highly organized: there were committees on law, on sociology, education, sci- ence, arts and letters and women's work in industry. The committees accepted proposals from subcommittees; those which seemed feasible were to be presented formally to the general assembly at the conclusion of the Congress. Voting rights were reserved for delegates from more than fifty or- ganizations, the members of which could attend committee sessions and general assembly meetings. This careful or- ganization was applauded by the Argentine press, many of whom had not believed that women were capable of or- ganizing so professional a convention.[10]

Papers at the committee sessions traced the progress women had made in social work and education, the two fields most accessible to them. Non-elite philanthropies put together the sessions on female industry and the preserva- tion of native crafts, while members of the Feminist Centers reported on technical education.[11] The "sociological" sessions were catch-alls for assorted topics: for instance, the importance of feminism as a means of abolishing hostility between the sexes; and the necessity of legal abolition of duelling — which, incidentally, was responsible for at least ten deaths a year in Argentina until the 1930s.

The delegates had no difficulty coming to complete agreement about the need for co-educational schools where both sexes would learn a single moral standard; and the need for more kindergartens, expanded physical education, improved teacher training and special schools for handicapped children. They deplored what they called "empty patriotism" and asked that students be taught the history of their ancestral countries as well as Argentine history: this resolution reflected the European backgrounds of over half the delegates and the bias toward internationalism which evolved at least partly from their socialist sympathies. Ironically, this attitude contrasted with that of North American feminists who emphasized their patriotism and worked to help assimilate European immigrants to the United States.[12]

In the area of health and education there was agreement that child labor caused school truancy. The FIFC resolved that parents should be fined if their children were absent from school without good reason, and that working children should be required to attend school for a half day. In connection with children's health the women commented that it was hazardous to kiss and fondle babies excessively; this observation grew out of a general discussion of the problem of lack of discipline among the Argentine lower classes and the need to combat it with education on "scientific" mothering. These ideas reflected prevailing North American ideas on the subject.[13]

Questions about sexual conduct were settled by discussions of the need for males to attempt to control themselves and the necessity for the outlawing of prostitution, a familiar theme. The possibility of incest in crowded slum dwellings was touched upon. The question of the treatment of unwed mothers and their children was gone into more thoroughly than the preceding questions, because of the imminence of the establishment of the Children's House. Traditionally the orphanage run by the Beneficent Society was the depository for unwanted children. In some cases parents had planned to reclaim them when their economic difficulties were resolved but frequently the Society put the children up for adoption without notifying the natural parents.[14]

The FIFC officially disapproved of the Society's treatment of unwed mothers, preferring the Children's House, where poor women could stay and take care of their children, both legitimate and illegitimate, and be taught skills so that they could get jobs and take over the children's support themselves.[15] Union and Labor, an organization for feminist socialist workers, physicians and teachers was behind the establishment of the Children's House; they had founded a periodical (*Unión y Labor*) for the express purpose of establishing the Children's House and of uniting women to work for their civil rights. The organization offered community services for women and a platform for feminist discussion; the periodical, a record of feminist thought, argument and aspiration from 1910 to 1914, was an important organ for the international exchange of ideas between feminists.

Union and Labor had succeeded in persuading the provincial government of Buenos Aires to allocate funds to the Children's House. It had also helped to found the Argentine Temperance League, which listed among its supporters Alvina Van Praet de Sala,[16] who agreed with the feminists about alcohol, but not about the abolition of legalized prostitution which she held to be a protection against venereal disease for wives and a shield for young virgins against the sexual demands of their suitors. Union and Labor had tried and failed to bring about the cessation of mandatory physical examination of prostitutes by the National Department of Health.

Their primary effort was the Children's House. The board of Union and Labor required their professional members to devote several hours a week to the Children's House and a certain amount of time each week to the needs of poor women. In return the periodical ran free advertisements for the professional women, a practice that gave rise to some acrimony: the editors complained repeatedly that these women were attempting to further their own careers at the expense of Union and Labor.[17] The Socialist feminists were committed to working for a better world; personal ambition was anathema to them and women suspected of such tendencies were bitterly criticized and even ostracized. As late as 1977 Alicia Moreau de Justo called Julieta Lanteri an egoist and a self-seeking individualist.[18]

Agreement on the need for public funding for institutions similar to the Children's House, and indeed, for a new social welfare system dealing with the problem of child abandonment, was complete at the FIFC. But there was controversy on protective legislation, divorce, and the proper approach to the legal and political status of women.

Raquel Messina, a teacher and social worker from the Socialist Women's Center, presented eight main proposals, drawn up by Socialists, for the regulation of female and child labor: these included forty days of maternity leave with pay, seats for saleswomen in shops, and day care facilities in factories. Elvira Rawson and María Abela de Ramírez, representing respectively the Feminist Center and the National League of Women Freethinkers, dissented from these proposals because they feared their enactment would discourage the employment of women.[19] They pointed out that women could not demand equality and at the same time request a privileged position in the labor market. Dr Rawson suggested that the FIFC ask for improved working conditions for both men and women. She had no objection to special protective legislation for children.

Although Socialist women were the most powerful and unified bloc at the Congress, and the Socialist party itself was favored by most feminists, respect for Elvira Rawson's views caused the FIFC to reject the Socialist demand for protective legislation. Dr Rawson often acted as a mediator between conservative and liberal factions in the women's movement. She was an independent thinker who in 1892 had written a book in which she attempted to defend the actions of women who preferred brothel life to survival in Buenos Aires' factories and sweatshops.[20] She herself was a member of the Radical Party, probably only because her husband, Manuel Dellepiane, was a Radical leader, since the Radicals did not care at all about women's questions and in fact relegated women to an auxiliary association without voting privileges. Dr Rawson's compromise, which called for better conditions for all workers, meant in effect that the women would support the ineffectual legislation now on the books, but rejected stronger laws. The FIFC endorsed this compromise; the Socialists were not of course affected by it, and the party continued to work for national protective legislation for women.

More controversy was sparked by a speech by Carolina Muzzilli, in which she blamed lack of legal divorce for adultery, child abuse and prostitution. In 1907 divorce had been legalized in Uruguay, and the "social equilibrium" of Argentina, Carolina Muzzilli said, demanded the enactment of divorce laws there too.[21] Once more Elvira Rawson dissented. She expressed doubt about the quick reform of traditional institutions; she feared such actions could lead to abuse. She was particularly concerned about the welfare of the children of divorced parents, and about the situation of women in a country where divorce was legal, but where they had no constitutional protection. She reminded the

Congress that courts in Argentina tended to favor the claims of men over those of women.[22] She would support a resolution on divorce only if it contained certain restrictions. The Socialists Sara Justo and María Abela de Ramírez insisted that an unrestricted divorce law was part of the civil reform which women must achieve. Divorce, they said, must be a civil right like any other civil right.

Divorce of any kind was flatly rejected by the relatively few devout Catholics at the Congress, of whom Atilia Canetti de Rosales, a 1908 graduate of the University of Buenos Aires and a leader of the Argentine Association against the White Slave Trade, was the most outspoken. Her arguments did not convince the delegates, who accepted Elvira Rawson's position on divorce. There was a general distrust of pious women among the Socialists and freethinkers; fairly or unfairly, it was believed that women were far more susceptible than men to the influence of the Church, and this was, in fact, one of the arguments used by those opposed to woman suffrage. It was feared that women's votes would largely rubber-stamp the desires of the Church and give it more influence in political affairs. This point was raised at the Congress.

The women from the AAFT and the Feminist Center wanted the Congress to make an official protest about the exclusion of women from the political process. But other delegates were opposed to this: they felt that before suffrage could be broached, women must change their civil status: they were legal minors who could not administer their own property, testify in court or make decisions about their children. The suffragists chose Ana Montalvo, a teacher from the AAFT in Rosario, to plead their cause. She ran through the familiar bitter argument about the poor judgement of the enfranchised, pointing to the present Argentine government to prove her point: "Could women do any worse?"

Certainly, if one could tolerate political ignorance in

men, one could tolerate it also in women. Ana Montalvo said she had no objection to qualified suffrage; in fact she wanted it to be extended to women. She attempted to refute all the standard arguments against woman suffrage, one of which was the inability of women to serve in the army. Women, she said, provided the children who fought the wars; surely that was proof enough of their patriotism? And did this argument then mean that disabled men who could not serve in the military should also lose the franchise?[23] On behalf of the AAFT she presented several resolutions on women's rights which the majority approved in principle, since they believed that they would eventually work for woman suffrage. But they rejected the AAFT proposal that the Congress draft a woman suffrage bill to be included with pending universal suffrage legislation. To Socialist feminists, the goals of the Socialist party had to come first and they were afraid that politicians would be alienated by excessive demands by women.[24] After universal manhood suffrage was enacted, the Socialist feminists believed that male Socialist politicians would be elected who could then work with them on woman suffrage. The party needed first of all to get a foothold in Buenos Aires by electing their candidates who could work on reforms; and in fact after 1915 when they had won several seats in the Chamber of Deputies, the Socialists presented a bill for woman suffrage in almost every legislative session, although Juan B. Justo himself believed that Argentine political institutions were too reactionary to tolerate any reform of women's status.

In the closing days of the FIFC the delegates resolved that the women of Latin America should pursue the question of equal rights at some future time, but that they should work vigorously for the improvement of the lives of women and children. This last goal was not a controversial one; it was something that the NCW could wholeheartedly endorse. Obviously not wishing to make any binding decisions at the Congress, the delegates resolved to meet in Chile in 1913 to evaluate the progress of the women's movements in each Latin American country and establish goals at that time.[25] This meeting never took place, doubtless because of the sporadic commitment of Argentine feminists to their cause. This, in turn, might well have been because they did not, as feminists in Europe and the United States did, focus their energies upon suffrage. Without this single, clear, unifying goal the movement dissipated its energies.

Notes

[1]Gina Lombroso, *The Soul of Woman: Reflections on Life* (NY: Dutton, 1910), p. 37.

[2]*La Prensa*, April 20, 1910; May 10, 1910.

[3]Celia La Palma de Emery, *Acción pública y privada en favor de la mujer y del niño* (BA: Alfa y Omega, 1910), p. 36.

[4]Hollander, p. 194.

[5]Little, "Education, Philanthropy and Feminism", p. 244; Delfina Bunge de Gálvez, *Las mujeres y la vocación* (BA: Editorial Piblet, 1952).

[6]Sara Justo, *Movimiento femenino en Europa*, p. 6.

[7]*Unión y Labor* I no. 9 (June 21, 1910), 19-20.

[8]*Primer Congreso Femenino Internacional de la República Argentina* (BA: Alfa y Omega, 1910), pp. 5-156.

[9]*Primer Congreso*, López speech, pp. 4-48.

[10]*La Prensa*, 18-23 May, 1910.

[11]*Primer Congreso*, pp. 8-24.

[12]William O'Neill, *Everyone Was Brave: A History of Feminism in America* (Chicago: Quadrangle Press, 1971).

[13]Christine Stansell, "Women, Children and the Uses of the Streets; Class and Gender Conflicts in New York City, 1850-1860", *Feminist Studies* VIII, no 2 (Summer, 1982), 309-336.

[14]Little, p. 246.

[15]*Unión y Labor*, I, no 1, 7.

[16]*Estatutos de la Liga Nacional de Templanza de la República Argentina* (BA: 1922).

[17]*Unión y Labor* IV, no 38 (Nov., 1912), 16

[18]Author's interview with Alicia Moreau de Justo, 1 Aug., 1977.

[19]*Primer Congreso*, p. 416-424.

[20] Elvira Rawson, *Apuntes sobre higiene de la mujer* (BA: 1892).

[21]*Ibid*, p. 426.

[22]*Ibid*, p. 425.

[23]*Primer Congreso*, Montalvo speech, pp. 409-415.

[24]*Unión y Labor*, 1909-1913.

[25]*Primer Congreso*, p. 415.

8

War's Aftermath, 1918-1926

> The task of the International Woman's Suffrage Alliance is the awakening of women to their national duties and responsibilities in those countries which have not yet entrusted their women with political freedom.
>
> Carrie Chapman Catt, 1920[1]

In 1912 the Sáenz Peña Law, named after Roque Sáenz Peña, the progressive conservative President of the Republic, was passed, establishing universal compulsory male suffrage for citizens over eighteen years of age, and causing great political change in the country. Seventy to eighty percent of the electorate turned out and the party which profited the most was not Sáenz Peña's conservative faction, but the Radical party, a group identified only with popular democracy and vague political reform. Under Hipólito Yrigoyen the Radicals took advantage of regional division in the conservative ranks and made much headway, probably because their platform was vague enough to appeal to the landed oligarchy as well as to the urban and rural middle class. Consequently in 1916, by a majority of only one vote in the electoral college, Yrigoyen attained the presidency. Thus suffrage reform catapulted the former rebels to power, where Yrigoyen was to remain until October of 1922. During that time there were a series of battles between conservatives and Radicals, even though the Radicals wanted only mild reforms and were basically conservative themselves.[2]

Yrigoyen's victory encouraged the feminists, who had had little contact during World War I with women in the rest of the world; they believed that issues of concern to women would now get a sympathetic hearing. The establishment of the League of Nations was a positive sign: it would encourage internationalism and the exchange of ideas so valuable to Argentine feminists. And women in English-speaking countries appeared to be on the brink of receiving the vote in recognition of their contributions to the war effort.

The women's movement in the United States did indeed develop swiftly after the War. In 1915 Carrie Chapman Catt (1859-1947) assumed the presidency of the National American Women's Suffrage Association (NAWSA), in which membership had increased from seventeen thousand in 1905 to seventy-five thousand in 1910. In 1913, when Theodore Roosevelt's Progressive Party, which had endorsed woman suffrage, began to dissolve, other politicians expressed support for suffrage, hoping to attract Progressive votes for the national elections in 1914. After the United States entered the War, Mrs Catt pointed constantly to the contributions women were making to the war effort through factory work, nursing and fundraising. At the same time she avoided being linked with militant suffragists whose behavior alienated the public. Undoubtedly as a result of all this, by the end of 1917 NAWSA had grown to two million members and in 1919 the Senate sent the Nineteenth Amendment to the states for consideration; in 1920 it was ratified by the required three-quarters of the states, giving women the vote at last.[3]

Things were not to go that smoothly for the Latin American women's movement in the years right after the War, although several new organizations were founded by energetic and optimistic feminists. In 1916 Paulina Luisi (1875-1950) organized the NCW in Montevideo, Uruguay, which was the most progressive nation in Latin America, having been colonized at a relatively late date and being, by 1900, largely a land of European immigrants. Divorce had been legalized in 1907 and the Civil Code reformed to benefit women. Although the women who joined the Uruguayan NCW were largely upper class, the organization worked wholeheartedly for woman suffrage and social reform, undoubtedly buoyed by the continuing influence of Paulina Luisi. She and her sisters came from an affluent German-Italian family, were among the first women in Uruguay to obtain a university education and she herself was the first woman in Uruguay to earn a medical degree.[4]

Dr Luisi was a friend of Alicia Moreau de Justo who, in 1918, founded the National Feminist Union in Buenos Aires to attract working-class women to the Socialist party which supported suffrage and reform of the Civil Code. The four hundred members of the Union prepared a suffrage bill and obtained eight thousand signatures in support of it.[5] The bill suffered the usual fate of Argentine woman suffrage bills, but Dr Moreau and her associates were gratified by what they perceived as a positive public response.

In that year of 1918 two other women's rights groups were organized: the Women's Rights Association, by Elvira Rawson de Dellepiane, and the National Feminist Party, by Julieta Lanteri. Dr Rawson de Dellepiane's organization was made up of women from the Feminist Center, the AAUW, women's auxiliaries of the Radical party, and even the NCW. Catholic women felt comfortable with Dr Rawson, whose husband was a Radical politician, even though she herself was not religious. She was one of the few activists who was able to bridge the gap between factions of the Argentine woman's movement. She came from an elite background, had no difficulty maintaining friendly contact with the NCW and was not an ideologue. Although she admired the determination of feminists like the Pankhurst sisters in England, she, like Carrie Chapman Catt, believed that their militancy was counterproductive.[6] The last thing she wanted was a battle between feminists, the Church and the Establishment. She endorsed the NCW position that women should have their civil rights before they attempted the franchise. She believed that this position enabled her to build the WRA from a few dozen members to eleven thousand by the 1930s.

Julieta Lanteri, like Elvira Rawson and Alicia Moreau, was a medical doctor; the main concern of her National Feminist Party was the franchise. She and a small group of professional women had been planning a suffrage campaign since 1911; now, in 1918, the climate seemed to them to be favorable. As we have seen, Dr Lanteri had the franchise because she was married to a prominent Argentine citizen; between 1911 and 1916 she voted in every election in the province of Buenos Aires. But in 1916 the provincial legislature made military service a prerequisite for suffrage, thus effectively disenfranchising all women, and incidentally, some men.[7] This snub helped to spur the formation of the National Feminist Party.

Dr Lanteri wanted to call attention to the exclusion of women from the political process, so in 1919 she had ten male supporters present her name to the local election officials and began a campaign for the office of national Deputy, knowing she could not possibly win.[8] Although suffrage and civil rights legislation had failed once more, debates on the subject in the Chamber of Deputies had aroused public interest, or so it seemed to those concerned.

In that same year Alicia Moreau de Justo expended much time and energy travelling to organize feminists in the provinces and in other Latin American countries. To a large extent, this effort was fruitless. She and Paulina Luisi organized short-lived groups in the Argentine cities of Santa Fe and Córdoba; Dr Moreau spent three weeks in Chile meeting with feminists in Santiago and Valparaiso: Amanda Labarca de Hubertson, the leader of the Chilean feminists, had pledged to work with Dr Luisi and Dr Moreau to build a united suffrage movement in the southern cone of South America. Although they were to invest twenty years of work in this project, it too was doomed to failure.[9]

On the way to the United States for a two month visit, Dr. Moreau paused in Peru and Mexico, where there was no feminist activity at all; the only women's organizations were large Catholic philanthropies. Dr Moreau was visiting the U.S. to address the International Congress of Women Workers and the International Congress of Women Doctors which she had helped to found, and to meet with Carrie Chapman Catt. In Washington, she spoke to the Women Workers about the activities of the Argentine Socialist party and its work with women, and she was made honorary vice president of the international organization.[10] Her agenda for women workers included government-sponsored day care centers, comprehensive maternity protection, equal pay and a forty-four hour work week. At the International Congress of Women Doctors, she discussed the evils of prostitution and the white slave trade in Buenos Aires.[11] She discussed also the failure of feminists' attempts to set up compulsory sex education in the public schools and in the army. Only when women had the vote, she said, could these reforms be instituted. Woman suffrage was not an end in itself, but a means to an end, which women should demand not for themselves but for the sake of future generations.

At the end of her visit, Dr Moreau went to New York to spend several days with Carrie Chapman Catt, to whom she explained that her National Feminist Union was opposed to qualified suffrage, despite the fact that many Argentine feminists, including her sister-in-law Sara Justo, believed that qualified suffrage was the only suffrage Argentine women were likely to get, and Dr Moreau acknowledged that many European feminists had no objection to qualified suffrage. The Argentine Chamber of Deputies seemed to hold out the possibility that they would consider it, and Dr Moreau suspected that Elvira Rawson was open to it, although she had not said so. Mrs Catt agreed that setting property and educational qualifications for the vote was unfair and undemocratic but IWSA intended to leave such matters to the judgment of its member organizations in each country.

Alicia Moreau wanted to know IWSA positions on various issues, but most of all she wanted Mrs Catt's support; she wanted her to come to Buenos Aires in 1921 for the Pan American Congress to help conduct a strong campaign for woman suffrage. Mrs Catt was impressed with the Argentine feminists' dedication in a hostile political and social environment; she suggested a regular correspondence and an exchange of periodicals. For the next few years Dr Moreau received the IWSA magazine *The Woman Citizen* and reciprocated with *Our Cause* (*Nuestra Causa*), the periodical of the National Feminist Union which Dr Moreau made a member of IWSA.

In 1920, an election year, the National Feminist Union decided to try running a mock election campaign simultaniously with the congressional campaigns in March. The idea was borrowed from French suffragists who had held a mock election in Paris in 1918 to gauge public support for woman suffrage. Julieta Lanteri was already running for office with the support of the National Feminist Party, and Elvira Rawson's Women's Rights Party was willing to work with the National Feminist Union, so all three new feminist organizations would be taking part in the mock election. They were, however, not unified in any other way, except for their ultimate goals. As we have seen, Dr Moreau disliked what she called Dr Lanteri's "individualism"; she saw the latter's election campaign as self-seeking, since she believed that Dr Lanteri should have worked with the two groups instead of attempting to establish a political base for herself.[12] Dr Lanteri, in her turn, did not want to work with groups which were supporting, respectively, male Socialists and Radicals as well as the suffrage issue. She wanted to work only for women; her object in the mock election was to prove that women were capable of fielding candidates and voting for them, since opponents of suffrage had questioned women's ability to do that.[13] And Dr Lanteri believed that Dr Moreau had compromised her own principles by joining with Elvira Rawson, since many members of Dr Rawson's Women's Rights Association were willing to accept qualified suffrage.

Dr Moreau wanted a well-conducted, dignified campaign; Dr Lanteri, however, created a sensation. She received attention from the North and South American press, as well as daily notice from the Buenos Aires newspapers, which even turned meeting rooms over to her. Since many women from the British community were working with her, the *Buenos Aires Herald* followed her campaign closely. Dr Moreau could not have been happy to see that, although all three organizations had specifically dissociated themselves from the actions of militant North American and English suffragists, the *Herald* called Dr Lanteri "the Pankhurst of Argentina".[14]

Her campaign attracted so much attention that Katharine Dreier, a New York feminist, came to Buenos Aires to observe the election. Although Katharine Dreier admired Dr Moreau and Paulina Luisi, who had come from Uruguay to work with the National Feminist Union, she was most impressed with Julieta Lanteri, who alone was willing to subject herself to the insults of the citizens of Buenos Aires by campaigning in subway stations and parks, as well as on street corners and in other public places.[15]

In early March her appearance in a public park in the Flores district created the first outdoor suffrage rally in South America. Two thousand people filled the park; Dr Lanteri, who was barely five feet tall, had to stand on a bench to address the crowd. A goodly number of the audience had come to jeer at her, so even her powerful voice could hardly be heard at times. She remained calm and even appeared amused at some comments. To a man who cried out that women should not vote because they needed to take care of their children, Dr Lanteri replied, "What foolishness, what nonsense . . . ! Who will take care of the children, the eternal argument . . . in all countries! You never ask that question when you employ women in your factories, and far more women work in factories than could ever fill the Chamber of Deputies."[16]

Katharine Dreier, who went to Dr Lanteri's rallies with Alicia Moreau, was caught up in the excitement:

> I liked the group of men who were backing Dr Lanteri-Renshaw. It was a satisfaction to come in actual contact with Argentine men who respected women and who wanted to further their interests in every way. It was a brave stand for these men to take, and yes, in this curious city where personality counts for so much, the class of men who had risen to . . . promote this candidate was such that soon the laugh was silenced. A little incident is worth relating. Curiously enough, Dr Lanteri-Renshaw entered the same subway train as Dr Moreau and myself on our homeward trip. We soon held a little suffrage meeting right then and there . . . A group of well-to-do uneducated people began to snicker, but when they saw the men whom they respected, the men of position and dignity, were listening with interest and congratulating Dr Lanteri-Renshaw, as well as Dr Moreau and myself, their attitude turned to one of respect . . . Dr Lanteri-Renshaw's meetings continued to grow and so popular did she become that seven cinematographs put their houses at her disposal to speak between films . . . [17]

Dr Lanteri's platform, which was distributed at rallies and meetings and widely throughout the city, was a summary of the goals sought by the Argentine feminists:

LEGISLATION

Universal suffrage for both sexes; Civil equality for all sexes; Civil equality for legitimate and illegitimate children; Acknowledgement of the mother as functionary of the State; Tutelage of orphans and abandoned children; Absolute divorce.

WORK

Six hours the maximum of work for women; Equal pay for equal work; Protection laws for working women and children; Old age pensions for all workers and employees; Pensions for the aged; Rest and wages for all women during pregnancy and the nursing period.

EDUCATION AND JUSTICE

Mother Culture; Professional co-education in industrial art, agriculture and household economics; Colonies for the feeble-minded, blind, deaf and dumb; Colonial reformatories for incorrigible boys, backward and delinquent children; Women prison reforms . . . Abolition of capital punishment; Tribunals for children in separate buildings.

SOCIAL HYGIENE

Creation of a council for social hygiene and prophylactic treatment of infectious diseases; Laws about safety devices in factories; Sanitaria for alcoholics; Abolition of the sale, manufacture or importation of alcoholic drinks; Abolition of regulated houses of prostitution; Proportional representation of the minority in the national, provincial and municipal governments.[18]

Julieta Lanteri was not surprised to encounter difficulties during her campaign; what did surprise her and her colleagues was the indifference of women to the calls of suffrage and reform. The greatest enemy of the woman suffrage movement, she said a few days before the election, was female indifference.[19] Without the help of liberal men, she said, she could not have waged her campaign.

On the day before the election the Buenos Aires press attacked the women's mock election, and on election day itself there were some sporadic outbursts of hostility. One father forcibly prevented his daughter from casting her ballot. On the following day the *Buenos Aires Herald*, which had appeared sympathetic, accused the feminists of fomenting demonstrations.[20]

On election day the National Feminist Union set up polling places in all twenty of Buenos Aire's electoral districts, which were supervised by members of the three suffrage groups.[21] The locations of these polling places were published in *La Prensa* and *La Nación* for days before the election, but only four thousand women cast their votes. Since Alicia Moreau's Socialist organization had managed to recruit working-class women to vote, the National Feminist Union made the best showing, with two thousand votes. Next came Julieta Lanteri who received votes in all districts amounting to approximately one thousand three hundred. Last came Elvira Rawson's Radicals with about seven hundred votes.[22]

The women, especially Julieta Lanteri, were disheartened by this poor showing. And in fact the atmosphere in Buenos Aires in 1920 was too volatile to allow a dispassionate consideration of the women's case. The Radical government was engaged in a struggle with the Socialists for the loyalty of the working class. In 1918 the Radicals won a congressional victory because of their benign attitude toward strikers in the preceding two years. This pro-labor stance outraged the conservatives, who began to work with various businessmen's organizations to form the National Labor Association (*Asociación Nacional del Trabajo*) to fight the unions. This situation, along with high inflation and a drop in wages, led in January 1919 to what was to be known as "The Tragic Week".

This began in 1918 in Buenos Aires with a strike of metallurgical workers whose livelihood had been badly damaged by the World War. The strike became violent. When the police intervened, a policeman was killed and two days later in the ensuing fighting five bystanders died. After that everything went out of control. On 9 January, 1919, there was a general strike, dotted with violence; the Radicals bowed to conservative rage and the army was called out, after which gangs of vigilantes roamed the streets hunting for "Bolsheviks" and "troublemakers" and attacking people freely, especially Russian Jews. These vigilantes later created a right-wing organization calling itself the Argentine Patriotic League, which was to remain in existence as one of the most powerful political organizations in the country for the next few years, intimidating the government if it attempted in any way to appeal to unions and relying for support upon the army. Frightened by the real possibility of a coup, Yrigoyen did not attempt to interfere with them.[23]

As the economy showed signs of recovery after 1919, Yrigoyen began to spend money for patronage to build support, a tactic which succeeded in the 1920 elections. However, the general atmosphere was not conducive to reform; and the women were disheartened not only by their poor showing in the March elections, but by the defensive stance which they were forced by their opponents to assume.

They were not surrounded completely by hostility, of course. A male lawyer named Miguel Font organized sympathetic politicians and professional men into the League for the Defense of Women's Rights and in 1921 published a book on the subject containing interviews with prominent people, both male and female. Not all the respondents were feminists by any means. Indeed, one of them was Manuel Carlés, one of the founders of the Argentine Patriotic League, who not only wished to prevent women from voting but decried universal male suffrage, which he believed had opened the door to all sorts of dangerous elements.[24] The Patriotic League wanted restriction and not expansion of the franchise.

The League was not motivated by misogyny. On the contrary, they asked women to help prevent social upheaval by discouraging their husbands and children from exposing themselves to the seductive appeal of leftist foreign ideas. Women of all classes, they believed, were the foundation of the family and the custodians of the Argentine creole values of nationalism and Catholicism. "Red feminism", the League held, had been fomented by the atheistic public school system; the feminists were trying to wean women from tradition so that Argentina would become like western Europe and the United States.[25]

The Beneficent Society had no quarrel with this position. Several NCW members, among them Celia La Palma de Emery, helped to organize a women's branch of the Argentine Patriotic League. Among the League's goals was the Argentinization of women workers, and to this end they organized vocational educational classes for working-class girls and arranged for Catholic masses to be held in factories. They worked, they said, for "moral education": they wished to help poor working women to improve their lives, and at the same time to understand the importance of patience and courtesy, of obedience to the law and to one's superiors, and of duty to one's country and to one's family.[26]

These goals were more or less the same as the goals of the Social Catholic movement, the Church's response, worldwide, to the challenges of liberalism and social unrest. The leaders of this movement in Argentina during the first forty years or so of this century were the priests Miguel de Andrea and Gustavo J. Franceschi. To counteract leftist influences, they organized Catholic trades unions for women workers. In 1931 Father de Andrea said that seven thousand women belonged to his worker syndicates.[27]

Thus, despite their obvious differences, both Catholic conservatives and leftists saw the need for social action to alleviate poverty and women's working conditions. Tomas Amadeo, a conservative Catholic, whose Argentine Social Museum researched ways that philanthropists and social workers could solve social problems, received cooperation from feminist social workers and educators as well as from Catholic charities. All were agreed that protective legislation was necessary.[28] In 1924 feminists, anti-feminists, liberals, and conservatives banded together to support the passage of legislation regulating the non-agricultural work of women and children, a reworked version of the unimplemented law of 1907 which had been presented to the Congress by the Socialist deputy Alfredo Palacios.

Law 11.317 limited work for women to eight hours a day and forty-eight hours a week, and outlawed night work for women under eighteen years old, except for domestics and entertainers. The age restriction was an attempt to eradicate adolescent prostitution. In addition, women and children could not be hired for dangerous or unhealthy work. If employers broke the law they were subject to damages. Limited maternity protection was included.

During the time the law was being debated the feminists behaved with great restraint. So proper was their demeanor that Alicia Moreau de Justo was allowed to present the feminist position before the Chamber of Deputies. Alicia Moreau and Elvira Rawson hailed the law's enactment as a victory for feminists, despite its flaws and the lack of any mechanism for enforcement. At the time protective legislation of this kind was seen as an enormously progressive step; it was only many years later when unions grew in power and influence that feminists realized that special legislation effectively pushed women out of the labor mainstream and out of higher-paid jobs.[29]

Encouraged by this accomplishment, in 1925 the Argentine feminists joined with some Radicals, Socialists and conservatives to attempt a reform of the Civil Code. A coalition of congressmen were willing to push such legislation through both houses; even the NCW supported extensive Code reform for married women. The National Feminist Union and the Women's Rights Association worked smoothly with the NCW to avoid any appearance of aggressiveness or any attempt to connect Civil Code reform with suffragism. As a result the desired legislation was passed in 1926.

Adult married women were granted equal civil rights with adult men; unwed mothers were granted parental rights over their children; married women were given the right to enter professions and dispose of their earnings without their husbands' consent and to enter into civil contracts. Widows were granted authority over their children and over the estates of minor children, whether these women remarried or not. However, Article Six of the new law stipulated that women must demand these civil rights through legal action if they had no prenuptial agreements. Unless the wife demanded her share of conjugal property through the courts, the husband continued to be the legal holder of this property and had no obligation to share it.[30]

Article Six naturally led to the establishment of women's centers by women lawyers in Buenos Aires and several provincial capitals, since the mass of women undoubtedly either had no idea that they had been granted any rights, or had no way of suing for these rights.

Thus the Argentine feminists could claim a few victories in the 1920s. The climate in the country was obviously not receptive to their cause, however; they had been able to build no mass base. They entered the following decade in an optimistic mood, although there was to be no improvement at all in the general perception of their programs.

Notes

[1]*Woman Citizen*; vol. 4, no. 5 (June, 1920), 692.

[2]See David Rock, *Argentina 1516-1982*, pp 183-190.

[3]See Evans, *Feminists*, p. 241, *Woman Citizen*, vol. 4, no. 5 (10 June, 1920), 692.

[4]Consejo Nacional de Mujeres del Uruguay, *Estatutos y reglamentos* (Montevideo: "El Siglo Ilustrado" de G.U. Marino, 1917), pp. 1-12; Paulina Luisi, *Movimiento Sufragista* (Montevideo: "El Siglo Ilustrado" de G.U. Marino), pp. 2-20.

[5]*Buenos Aires Herald*, 7 Sept., 1920.

[6]*Ibid*, 4 Jan., 1920.

[7]Cocca, *Sufragio femenino*, p. 16.

[8]*Buenos Aires Herald*, 4 March, 1920.

[9]Author's interview with Alicia Moreau de Justo, 1 Aug., 1977.

[10]*La Razón*, 29 Sept., 1919.

[11]Alicia Moreau, "The White Slave Trade" in *Proceedings of the Internat'l Conf. of Women Doctors*, 1919, pp. 74-81.

[12]Moreau, *La mujer en la democracia*, p. 262.

[13]Ernesto Quesada, *El Feminismo Argentino: tendencias y orientaciones* (BA Talleres Gráficos Argentinos L. J. Rossi, 1920), p. 6.

[14]*Buenos Aires Herald*, 4 March, 1920.

[15]Katharine Dreier, *Five Months in the Argentine from a Woman's Point of View* (NY: Frederick Fairchild Sherman, 1920), pp 225-227.

[16]*Ibid*, p. 226.

[17]*Ibid*, p. 224.

[18]*Ibid*, pp. 230-231.

[19]*Buenos Aires Herald*, 2 March, 1920.

[20]*La Prensa*, 7 March, 1920.

[21]*Buenos Aires Herald*, 8 March, 1920.

[22]Dreier, pp. 233-234; Hollander, p. 227; *La Prensa*, 25 March, 1920. Figures from these three sources vary slightly.

[23]See Sandra McGee Deutsch, *Counterrevolution in Argentina, 1900-1932:* (Lincoln: Univ. of Nebraska Press, 1986).

[24]Miguel Font, *La mujer encuesta feminista Argentina* (BA: 1921).

[25]*Ibid*; See Carl Solberg, *Immigration and Nationalism in Argentina and Chile, 1890-1914* (Austin: Univ. of Texas, 1970); Marysa Gerassi, "Argentine Nationalism of the Right" Diss. Columbia Univ., 1964.

[26]Deutsch, pp. 89-91.

[27]Federación de Asociaciones Católicas de Empleadas, "Una visita a la casa de la empleada" in the archives of La Asociación Cristiana Femenina (BA: 1932).

[28]Deutsch, p. 155.

[29]Author's interview with Alicia Moreau de Justo, 3 Aug., 1977 and with Jorgelina Lozada, 16 July, 1977.

[30]*Boletín Mensual del Museo Social Argentino, 1911-1930;* Departamento Nacional del Trabajo, *Crónica Mensual* (Sept., 1924), vol. 7, p. 81; Mario Bravo, *Derechos civiles de la mujer* (BA: 1932), pp. 8-12, 226-239; Alfredo Colmo, *Derechos civiles de la mujer ante la experiencia* (BA: Talleres Gráficos Tudor, 1929), p. 9.

9

Argentina Turns to the Right

Yrigoyen's successor in 1922 was Marcelo T. de Alvear, a Radical from a wealthy landed family who, in an attempt to economize, alienated his party by wholesale firings of Yrigoyen's political appointees. The Radicals split, with the majority supporting Yrigoyen and beginning a strong campaign for his election in 1928. The minority group, which called itself the Antipersonalist Radical Party, joined with the conservatives in dislike of Yrigoyen; this dislike was particularly strong in the army and in the provinces. However, he was very popular with the middle class and it seemed to many of his enemies that only a military coup would rid them of him. By 1927 several right-wing anti-Yrigoyen nationalist groups had coalesced into the New Republic movement.

Yrigoyen won the election in 1928 with about sixty percent of the vote, partly because he had campaigned vigorously against Standard Oil in Argentina. But by 1930 the effects were being felt of the Depression which had struck the previous autumn and the government felt it necessary to cut spending; the result was that jobs vanished and incomes fell. When prosperity went, Yrigoyen's political base went with it. On the sixth of September, 1930, with relative ease, a military rebellion overthrew Yrigoyen and destroyed democracy in Argentina.[1]

General José F. Uriburu, a leader of the Patriotic League, became president of the provisional government. His politics were anti-democratic and extremely nationalistic. His followers wanted to suspend the 1853 Constitution, abolish elections and political parties and give all power to the state. However these desires were blocked by a larger group of liberal conservatives in the revolutionary coalition, led by General Agustín P. Justo; they wished to return the government to what it was before Yrigoyen won election in 1916, to retain the Constitution and the trappings, at least, of representative democracy.

A few days after the coup, several thousand women marched down the Avenida de Mayo to the presidential palace to demonstrate their support for what they called the restoration of political order. These women were not asking for the franchise; they wanted to participate in the stabilization of Argentine society through their traditional roles as patriotic mothers and guardians of Catholic morality.[2]

Despite the somewhat daunting political atmosphere, feminists retained their optimism. In 1933 *Women's Life* (*Vida Femenina*), a new feminist magazine, announced that women should prepare themselves for their impending civic responsibilities.[3] Alicia Moreau estimated at the time that in two or three years women would be allowed to vote in national elections.[4] In 1932 the executive board of the NCW voted to support qualified, non-compulsory woman suffrage.[5]

There had been some encouraging developments in the previous decade: in 1921 qualified women in the province of San Juan had been given the right to vote in municipal elections; and in 1927 in Santa Fe province they had been enfranchised for both municipal and provincial elections. However, it must be remembered that family and community were considered the natural purview of women, and local politics were related to these because they dealt with education and health services. Federico Cantoni, the provincial governor of San Juan, had helped put through qual-

ified female suffrage because he wanted a "tame electorate"; one which could be easily influenced.[6]

In 1929 Ecuadorian women received the franchise with
no woman's movement behind them. In that same year
Argentine feminists were humiliated when the Socialist
Senator Mario Bravo's suffrage bill did not receive even the
courtesy of a debate. The mock election campaign of 1920
had aroused public antipathy, and, to complicate matters,
there was a division in the ranks of the Socialist feminists. In
1929 Sara Justo told a columnist from the popular magazine *Faces and Letters* (*Caras y Caretas*) that she supported
qualified suffrage for both sexes; illiterates, she said,
should not vote.[7] Alicia Moreau de Justo considered this an
indefensible position, a betrayal of the ideals of Juan B.
Justo, who had died in 1928. Women should not vote at all,
Dr. Moreau de Justo said, unless the vote were democratic.[8]
Although any dissension in the feminist ranks was only a
tempest in a teapot on the national level, feminist morale
was further depressed by it, and not helped by the realiza-
tion that it made little difference one way or the other to the
issue of woman suffrage, which was in abeyance. The only
bright spot for the women in 1929 was the admission for the
first time of a woman to the Buenos Aires Board of Trade.

In 1930 Alicia Moreau founded the Socialist Women's
Suffrage Committee, to little response, which was not surprising since, for one thing, the Socialists were out of step
with the intensely nationalistic mood of the country—their
free trade position, for example, opened them to accusations of wishing to sell the country to foreign powers—and,
for another, Alicia Moreau's mock election campaign had
connected her firmly in the public mind with rabble-rous-
ing and detested ideas imported from Europe and North
America. Although the Socialists gained enough votes from
a few urban districts to keep some Congressional seats, they
had no real base in Argentina after 1930.[9]

The only feminist group with any popular appeal was the

Argentine Association for Women's Suffrage, founded, also in 1930, by Carmela Horne de Burmeister (1881-1966), a *porteña* teacher and social worker who had been busy with her profession until the late '20s, had no political affiliation and who consequently escaped the hostility leveled at earlier suffragists. She carefully separated herself from other feminist organizations by stressing the patriotism and civic-mindedness of her group's members. She made it clear that suffrage was her only concern; AAWS had no political, religious or class bias. Its motto was "Fatherland, Civic Pride and Humanity."[10]

Undoubtedly for these reasons, the AAWS was more successful than other feminist organizations. By 1932 Carmela Horne de Burmeister claimed ten thousand members; by 1934, one hundred thousand. Branches were founded in the traditional Catholic provinces of Mendoza, Catamarca and Corrientes, as well, of course, as in Buenos Aires and Santa Fe provinces. Señora Horne de Burmeister knew how to use the press. For instance, in September of 1932, several days before suffrage was once more to be fruitlessly debated in the Chamber of Deputies, she arranged for Monseñor Gustavo Franceschi, a Social Catholic, and José Bustillo, a conservative Deputy, to discuss woman suffrage in a Buenos Aires theatre. Both men listened with respect to a rendition of the woman suffrage anthem, and made long speeches about the importance of the inclusion of women in the political life of the country.[11] Carmela Horne de Burmeister was the subject of frequent sympathetic newspaper articles and she and other AAWS representatives were often asked to address women's clubs and other civic associations. The organization distributed handbills in the street and circulated petitions, with quiet dignity.

The first open debate on woman suffrage took place in the Chamber of Deputies on September 15, and 16, 1932. The largely suffragist audience was at first threatened with expulsion from the gallery because of their enthusiastic response to speeches supporting their position; however these strictures were soon abandoned. The anti-suffragists talked about the excessive costs of setting up separate polling booths for women, whose modesty had to be protected, about the need for voters to serve in the military, and about the question of compulsory voting, which most delegates did not support for women.[12]

Late on the second day of discussion the Chamber passed a woman suffrage bill, leaving specifics to the conservative Senate where it was hoped there would be a speedy debate on the subject, but where in fact on September 20, the bill was tabled. It was not to be debated in the Senate until 1938, when it was defeated. In an unsigned article in the *Buenos Aires Herald*, the position was taken that women should be "granted a discreet and moderate use of their new political powers", postponing suffrage until they learned more about their "duties and responsibilities" toward the nation.[13]

Señora Horne de Burmeister responded to the tabling of the suffrage bill by attempting to stop debate in both houses on a pending divorce bill. She wrote a letter to the president of the Chamber of Deputies saying that it would be indefensible to pass a divorce bill when women were not allowed to vote on the issue, especially since one hundred thousand women had signed petitions expressing a desire for the franchise.[14] Nevertheless the divorce bill was debated and passed on September 24, 1932. Like the suffrage bill, it was tabled.[15] Divorce was not to be legalized in Argentina until November, 1986.

Carmela Horne de Burmeister's eventual goal, the building of a woman's party which would work for the general good, proved to be unattainable because first, women needed the franchise before they could think politically, and, second, most feminists at the time subordinated women's interests to Socialist ideology. When Señora Horne de Burmeister circulated a questionaire on suffrage among Buenos Aires women, she received one hundred and thirty-six thousand responses, the majority of which asked that the franchise be limited to "conscious, literate and adult women".[16] Alicia Moreau was particularly disappointed at these results; Señora Horne de Burmeister, while agreeing with Dr Moreau in principle, was willing to settle for qualified suffrage.

In 1932 a group called Patriotic Ladies was formed which supported gradual, qualified woman suffrage.[17] That same year Brazilian women, led by Bertha Lutz, won the right to vote after a fifteen-year struggle. And in Uruguay Paulina Luisi and the NCW achieved the franchise. Thus Argentina seemed to be slipping behind other Latin American countries,[18] although feminists were allowed a public forum on radio and in magazines: *Home* (*El Hogar*), a popular women's magazine, ran articles and advice columns on women's rights, but the editors' theme was generally "forward — but not too fast".[19]

By the 1930s the Argentine feminist leaders were growing old, and the movement was not attracting enough young women. One young woman who did join was Elena Bergman, Argentina's first woman economist, who thought that, on the whole, young women professionals did not connect suffrage with their own situations. In Rosario, her home province, women were more enlightened because there, she said, qualified women over the age of twenty-five could vote in municipal and provincial elections.[20] But new suffrage organizations continued to be founded: in 1933 the Association of Radical Ladies was formed as a feminist group for Radical women.

In 1934 Chilean women, led by Amanda Labarca de Hubertson, won the right to vote in municipal elections across the country. This was another blow to the Argentines: in southern South America, in those countries which had large middle-class European immigrant populations and a long commitment to liberalism, woman suffrage seemed imminent. Only Argentina appeared in this matter to be on a level with countries like Mexico, Paraguay and Peru, which had not had much European immigration and which were strongly controlled by the Church. But there was good news — albeit short-lived — for Argentine feminists in 1934: Dr Emar Acosta, from the province of San Juan, was elected to her provincial legislature, the first woman in the country's history to be elected to public office.[21] Dr Acosta had a law degree from the University of Buenos Aires, earned in 1927, and had been appointed assistant district attorney of San Juan by the provincial governor. In 1930 she resigned her post because she disagreed with what she considered the "anti-democratic" policies of the government, both national and provincial.

Despite this, and despite the fact that she had publicly denounced the violence of partisan politics, Dr Acosta was drafted as a candidate for the provincial legislature because of her "gentle but energetic" nature and her commitment to women's social welfare.[22]

She agreed to run because she wanted to work for the enforcement of protective legislation for women, passed in 1924, and because she believed that provincial women needed special education programs to help them assert their legal rights and also to protect themselves against venereal disease.[23] Although she was a devout Catholic who accepted state religion, she favored the abolition of religion in the schools and the legalization of divorce.[24]

After four months of service, Dr Acosta resigned, because she and eight other provincial legislators had been arrested by the San Juan police for breaking a quorum, the minimum number of legislators needed to conduct business. She refused to participate in a violent debate which destroyed the possibility of rational discussion. The other legislators, accustomed to the volatility of local politics, returned to their seats. Dr Acosta, however, held that she could not embroil herself in such uncivilized behavior, and that women should not be involved in that sort of thing. Her arrest, she said, was an unforgiveable offense against her dignity as a woman.[25] And indeed, most Argentine feminists believed that women should be a civilizing influence and remain above the fray.

In 1936 a further dampening fact emerged: a survey showed that sixty percent of Argentine women did not even know what enfranchisement meant.[26] But, nothing daunted, in that same year the feminists forged ahead: the Argentine Association of University Women became affiliated with the International Federation of University Women and held conferences on suffrage to attract young professional women; the NCW also opened a center for conferences on women's issues, but their somewhat "stuffy and aristocratic environment" did not generally appeal to professional women.[27] The YWCA (la Asociacion Cristiana Femenina) too served as a handy platform and gathering place for young working women and feminists.[28]

Nineteen thirty-six was a year filled with activity: President Franklin D. Roosevelt chose Buenos Aires as the site of the Pan American Peace Conference; his purpose was to create hemispheric solidarity against the threat of the European dictatorships, and he appealed directly to the Argentine delegation of the Pan American Peace Conference to join a Pan American defense alliance with the United States. But the Argentine government had encountered strong resistance to its attempts to export goods to the United States and Argentine feelings toward the U.S. were hostile, so Roosevelt's goal was not accomplished. Argentine feminists had been somewhat naively excited by the prospect of American participation in the Peace Conference, because Roosevelt was considered to be a strong supporter of women's rights. In addition, the experience of feminists with Pan American conferences had been positive; since World War I there had been a proliferation of these conferences dealing with world peace, women's civil and political rights, and the welfare of women and children.

In 1928 the Pan American Union had set up the Inter-American Commission on Women. But the feminists were not aware that Roosevelt wanted no distraction from the accomplishment of his goal of hemispheric solidarity, and in fact some members of the U.S. delegation had wanted the whole question of women's rights to be left off the agenda in Buenos Aires.[29] Nevertheless the Peace Conference of 1936 recommended that all governments adopt legislation granting to women full recognition of the rights and duties of citizenship.[30] But the Argentine foreign minister, Saavedra Lamas, who several years earlier had won the Nobel Peace Prize for his diplomatic endeavors during the Chaco War between Paraguay and Bolivia, declined to deliver the Argentine government's approval of woman suffrage.[31]

During the Peace Conference, Argentine female activists played host to the Inter-American Commission of Women, of which an Argentine woman, Ana Rosa Schlieper de Martínez Guerrero, had been named President. Carmela Horne de Burmeister, Alicia Moreau and Victoria Ocampo met with the leaders of the women's organizations from all American states; Doris Stevens, the North American leader of the Pan-American woman's movement, was one of the one hundred internationally prominent women who signed a petition for suffrage that was to be sent to the Argentine senate — again, it would evolve, in vain.[32]

Ana Rosa Schlieper de Martínez Guerrero, president of the Inter-American Commission on Women, had received this signal honor because of her philanthropic social work. In 1936 Señora Martínez Guerrero joined her friend the writer Victoria Ocampo, María Rosa Oliver and twelve other women to found the Union of Argentine Women, which offered a number of social and legal services for women, but which was founded primarily to campaign against changes in the Civil Code proposed by the administration of President Agustín P. Justo (1932-1938) — no relation to Juan and Sara Justo.[33]

These changes would, in effect, have revoked the reforms to the Civil Code enacted in 1926.[34] Married women would once again have the status of minors, unable to work outside their homes without the written permission of their husbands, unable to manage their own money or property, unable to join any commercial or civic organization. In addition President Justo introduced a bill which would require a government permit for any woman who wished to hire a wet nurse so that she could go out to work. The purpose behind this was the prevention of women's competition in the job market.[35]

Victoria Ocampo, as president of the Union of Argentine Women, enlisted the aid of Carmela Horne de Burmeister and Alicia Moreau de Justo to fight this legislation. Hundreds of women from all three organizations distributed thousands of handbills, held demonstrations and made statements to the press. Victoria Ocampo led a series of radio discussions on women's rights broadcast simultaneously in Argentina and Spain.[36] Public opinion was influenced to the degree that neither house of Congress would pass President Justo's proposed legislation.

Victoria Ocampo came from a privileged family. She and her sisters were educated by governesses; even the exclusive Catholic girls' schools of Buenos Aires were not good enough or exclusive enough for the Ocampos. Until she was twenty, she led a sheltered life. She wanted to be an actress, a career of which her father, Manuel Ocampo, strongly disapproved; she concentrated instead on becoming a serious writer; this ambition, too, displeased her family. When she was twenty-two she decided to free herself from the Ocampos by marrying. But the marriage, to Monaco Estrada, failed after only a few months because Victoria decided that she had exchanged one prison for another. She and her husband lived apart permanently after that, Victoria in an apartment in a fashionable district of Buenos Aires. She had an independent income and travelled often to Europe. In 1930 she founded *South* (Sur), a literary journal which contained work of European, North American and South American writers. Her friends included José Ortega y Gasset, Rabindranath Tagore, Paul Valéry, Maurice Ravel, Count Keyserling and André Gide. On one of her trips to England, she met Virginia Woolf, who had a strong effect upon her. She translated Mrs. Woolf's *A Room of One's Own* into Spanish.

The problems of Argentine women, she believed, stemmed from the inability of the older generation of women to encourage young women to develop their own personalities; there was no real friendship between women, but only competition for the attentions of men; and the only real female interests were courtship, marriage and mother-hood.

Toward the end of the thirties Victoria Ocampo lost interest in the Union of Argentine Women because some members — especially her friend María Rosa Oliver — began pressing for more political action; Victoria Ocampo was not really interested in politics; she wanted to devote her time to writing. Since her work had not found immediate popularity in Argentina she was eager to work for public acceptance of it. She was interested also in helping to rescue writers and other intellectuals from Hitler's Germany.[37]

After 1935 Victoria Ocampo and Alicia Moreau were the two most influential leaders of the Argentine women's movement. They shared the same general perspective. But they could not be entirely comfortable with each other. Alicia Moreau's life was dedicated to the egalitarian principles of democratic socialism. Victoria Ocampo, on the other hand, did not believe that a true levelling of society was either possible or desirable. She remained an aristocrat all her life.

By 1939 most women in the movement were focused on the war in Europe. Feminists shelved women's issues to work for peace organizations and later for war relief agencies. Ana Rosa Schlieper de Martínez Guerrero founded the Victory Committee, an Argentine women's war relief agency, and also joined the other feminists in Argentine Action, a group dedicated to an Allied victory in Europe and opposed to Argentine neutrality.

Thus in 1940 the Argentine feminist movement was at a virtual standstill. The suffrage bill sat in the Senate files and, even though the Supreme Court ruled that the Constitution did not deny women the vote, no action was taken. A presidential decree could have made woman's suffrage the law of the land, but the government was torn by various crises both internal and external. After decades of energetic lobbying, the suffragists were stalemated.

Notes

[1]See Joseph R. Barager, *Why Perón Came to Power* (New Brunswick: Rutgers University Press, 1967), p. 54. See also Goldwert, *Democracy, Militarism and Nationalism;* Jorge Abelardo Ramos, *Historia de la Nación Latinoamericana*, II (BA: A. Pena Lillo, 1973); Peter Snow, *Argentine Radicalism: The History and Doctrine of the Radical Civic Union* (Iowa City: Univ. of Iowa Press, 1965).

[2]*New York Times*, 16 Sept., 1930.

[3]*Vida Femenina*, 1 No 1 (9 Aug. 1933), 1.

[4]Author's interview with Alicia Moreau de Justo, 5 Aug., 1977.

[5]*La Nacíon*, 19 Jan., 1932.

[6]Anzoátegui, *La mujer y la historia*, p. 260; Alicia Moreau de Justo, *Cómo votar? Para que votar* (BA: Unión de Mujeres Socialistas, 1949), p. 7.

[7]"El voto femenino" in *Caras y Caretas*, XXXII: 1625 (23 Nov., 1929).

[8]Alicia Moreau de Justo, *El socialismo y la mujer* (BA: La Vanguardia, 1946).

[9]See Weinstein, *Juan B. Justo;* José Luis Torres, *La decada infame* (BA: Editorial Freeland), 1973.

[10]*El Hogar*, 21 Sept., 1934. See Carmela Horne de Burmeister, *Como se organizó el la Argentina el movimiento femenino en favor de los derechos politicos de la mujer por el Comité Argentino pro-voto de la asociación Argentina del sufragio femenino* (BA: Ricra y Cia., 1933), p. 1. Also *Asociación Argentina del sufragio femenino: fines y propósitos de los estatutos* (BA: 1932), p. 3.

[11]*La Nación*, 11 Sept., 1932.

[12]*Ibid*, 16 Sept., 1932. Aldo Armando Cocca, *Ley de sufragio femenino*, (BA: El Ateneo, 1948), pp. 105-123.

[13]*Buenos Aires Herald*, 20 Sept., 1932.

[14]Horne de Burmeister, Asociación, Argentina, p. 5.

[15]*Buenos Aires Herald*, 25 Sept., 1932.

[16]Horne de Burmeister, *Como se organizó*, p. 20.

[17]Lucila de Gregorio Lavié, *La ciudadana, para las mujeres que votan* (BA: Libro de Edición Argentina, 1948), p. 17.

[18]See the *Internat'l Women's Suffrage News, Equal Rights*, the *Pan American Magazine, Woman Citizen*, the *Woman's Journal*—periodicals of the '30s.

[19]*El Hogar*, 1930-1946.

[20]Author's interview with Elena Bergman, 15 Aug., 1977.

[21]Cocca, *Ley de sufragio femenino*, p. 128. Dr. Acosta won with 708 votes from women and 840 votes from men.

[22]*Bulletin of the Pan American Union* (Nov., 1934), p. 840.

[23]*Noticias Gráficas*, 28 July, 1934.

[24]*New York Times*, 29 July, 1934.

[25]*Ibid*, 10 Jan., 1935.

[26]Jorgelina Lozada, "Debe y quiere votar la mujer Argentina" in *La Novela Semenal* (3 March, 1936).

[27]Interview with Jorgelina Lozada, 10 Aug., 1977.

[28]Files of La Asociación Cristiana Femenina 1925-1943.

[29]Ruby Black, "The Americas for Equal Rights", *Equal Rights* (Mar., 1937), pp. 36-38.

[30]*Pan American Bulletin* (Feb., 1937), p. 108.

[31]For information on the 1936 Buenos Aires Peace Conference see Sally Ann Harris, "The Inter-American Peace Conference of the 1930's", Diss, Univ of Mo, 1967, Chapters 3 and 4.

[32]*Internat'l Women's News* (July, 1936), p. 79.

[33]*Unión Argentina de Mujeres, Memoria, 1936-1938* (BA: 1937).

[34]Unión Argentina, "Merecemos las mujeres este agravio? Proyecto absurdo de reforma del código civil," (BA: 1937). *Report on the Inter-American Commission on Women to the 18th Conf, of Amer. States on the Political and Civil Rights of Women.* (Lima, Peru: 1938), p. 15.

[35]Law 12. 341, *Pan American Bulletin* (June, 1937), pp. 500-501.

[36]Victoria Ocampo, *La mujer ye su expresión* (BA: Sur, 1936).

[37]See Doris Meyer, *Victoria Ocampo: Against the Wind and the Tide* (NY: Geo Braziller, 1979); Victoria Ocampo, *Testimonios I* (Madrid: Revista de Occidente, 1935); *Testimonios II* (BA: Sur, 1941); Victoria Ocampo, "Virginia Woolf in My Memory", transl. Doris Meyer, *Nimrod* (Spring/Summer 1956) pp. 142-150.

10

Feminism and the Peróns

> "I felt that the woman's movement in my country and all over the world had a sublime mission to fulfill . . . and everything I knew about feminism seemed to me ridiculous. For, not led by women but by those who aspired to be men, it ceased to be womanly and was nothing: feminism had taken the step from the sublime to the ridiculous. And that is the step I always try to avoid taking!"
>
> Eva Perón, 1951.[1]

In 1943 the conservative government of Ramon Castillo was overthrown by a coalition of military men calling itself the United Officers Group (GOU). There were various factions within the GOU, but basically they were opposed to communism and to foreign exploitation. General Arturo Rawson was declared President, but when he attempted to staff his cabinet with civilians, the GOU replaced him after only three days with General Pedro Ramírez, who had been Minister of War under Castillo. A considerable jockeying for power ensued in the Ramírez administration between strong nationalists and more liberal elements. The nationalists appeared to have the upper hand in October of 1943 when General Edelmiro Farrell, a firm nationalist, was promoted from Minister of War to Vice President and Enrique Martínez Zuvería, an anti-Semitic writer, became Minister of Justice and Public Instruction. Juan Domingo Perón (1894-1974), an army colonel from an immigrant middle-class background, who had been aide to Farrell, was made

Minister of Labor, and in June of 1944 became Minister of War.

The nationalist military government, strongly biased toward the Axis side in the second World War which was then raging, carried on a campaign for "moral purity" involving the censorship even of radio soap operas and tango lyrics, and the banning of the sales of contraceptives and of newspaper advertisements for Uruguayan divorce lawyers. Catholic religious instruction was made mandatory in all schools.[2] Anti-Nazi and pro-Ally organizations were shut down along with left-wing newspapers, including of course *La Vanguardia* the Socialist party organ which was closely allied to Argentine Action, a pro-Ally organization claiming seventy thousand members in 1943; Alicia Moreau de Justo, Victoria Ocampo and Ana Rosa Martínez de Guerrero sat on its board with forty-seven men, Ana Martínez de Guerrero also headed the Victory Committee, a similar women's organization labeled "subversive" by the government; in addition to its other failings it had been discovered to have sent clothes to war victims in Russia, breaking a law against supplying war relief to Communists. Along with having "harbored" Communists, the Committee was attacked for sending clothing overseas while many Argentine children were in rags.[3]

The government took the traditional position that women were morally superior to men, but all government employment above the status of clerk was closed to women, and students in girls' schools were required to memorize these words: "The Argentine woman should know how to jealously fulfill her natural obligations ... The dignity of woman consists in accepting her specific bodily functions ... The new Argentina wants pure, strong and clean women."[4]

The government and its nationalist newspapers were, in addition to being pro-Axis and anti-feminist, hostile to the oligarchy. For example, two provincial San Juan daily newspapers accused the leaders of Argentine Action and the

Victory Committee of being at the same time privileged members of the upper class and Russian Jews who were plotting a Communist takeover of the country. The upper class was seen as wishing to impose a non-Hispanic, basically Jewish Socialist order on the native Argentines; feminism was a foreign doctrine that threatened the core of Argentina's "spiritual Catholicism". Senora Martínez de Guerrero was accused of wearing "the overcoat of democracy" to hide the fact that she was a spy for "Russian devils."[5] In this hysterical atmosphere the cultural concept of "Hispanidad" — the rediscovery of Spain and its spiritual bond with its former colonies — developed into a powerful political concept for the Church, the army and the university, allied to Mussolini's Fascism with its emphasis on the cross and the sword.[6]

Along with its nationalism and hostility toward capitalism, the government had populist tendencies. Rural rents were reduced and an attempt was made to freeze rent and food prices in Buenos Aires. Juan Perón, in particular, was in a position to build a lower class constituency because of his control of the National Labor Department, the name of which he changed to the Secretariat for Labor and Social Welfare. The Secretariat collected statistics and other labor information; under Perón it was empowered for the first time to arbitrate strikes. Since the labor movement in Argentina had always been feeble, Perón could win the sympathy of the laboring classes with relatively little effort. In December of 1943 he was able to win a raise for the railroad workers, thus earning their undying gratitude. In 1944 he poured out a stream of legislation designed to improve the lives of workers; among other things, he established new labor courts. He involved himself in questions of pay, vacations, pensions, housing and accident compensation and received much publicity by intervening vigorously in strikes.[7]

The "descamisados" or "shirtless ones" responded to

Perón's rhetoric and his concrete efforts to improve their conditions. When, in June of 1944, he became Minister of War, his power increased. His new office gave him enormous leverage with the Army, since he now controlled promotions and supplies. His mentor, Edelmiro Farrell, was chosen by the Army early in 1944 to replace General Ramírez as president, moving Perón himself that much closer to the presidency. And Perón knew that reliance on military force alone could not keep the government in power; a popular base was a necessity for anyone who wished to challenge other members of the GOU. In particular, Perón recognized the value of winning the support of working class women, so far an untapped political resource. Unlike other Argentine politicians and military men, he understood that women could bolster a multi-class populist coalition. In 1943 women constituted one-quarter of the Argentine labor force. So Perón created a separate Women's Division at the Secretariat of Labor and promised that if he were president women of all classes would be recognized as first class citizens.[8]

In January of 1944 General Ramírez, under severe American pressure, including the threat of a total trade embargo, reluctantly broke off diplomatic relations with the Axis countries. Shortly afterward the Army replaced Ramírez with Edelmiro Farrell; in March of 1945 Argentina, again as a result of foreign pressure, declared war on Germany and Japan.[9] Immediately the Victory Committee revived and feminists from various organizations united in a new Woman's Pro-Suffrage Association, believing that their long wait was about to be rewarded. But to their surprise and deep chagrin they discovered instead that their cause was being preempted.

In 1945 Perón sent a petition to President Farrell asking for woman suffrage by presidential decree, since the Supreme Court had ruled that the Constitution did not deny women the right to vote. This proposal enraged the feminist leaders: they saw it as a cynical attempt to gain women's support for Perón's presidential ambitions, since the woman's movement had always been supported by the European-influenced left; from the nationalists had come only hostility. The feminists insisted that suffrage by presidential decree would be subject to annulment by the next holder of the office; they said that woman suffrage could be attained only by Constitutional amendment.[10] They formed a group called Democratico to fight Peron's suffrage proposal and his politics in general. Eugenia Silveyra de Oyuela, a feminist writer for La Nación, called Dr Lucila Gregorio de Lavié an opportunist, because Dr Lavié had accepted a high-level position in the Labor Secretariat and supported suffrage by decree.[11] Josefina Marpons, a Socialist feminist, accused Perón of planning "institutional anarchy" because of his request for a suffrage decree, and of trying to use women as "instruments" of his power.[12] Woman suffrage, the feminists said, should come about as a result of the "popular feminine will."[13]

For once the feminists were given cause to rejoice: Perón's petition was not successful, although it is doubtful that Democratico had anything to do with its rejection. Perón was not disturbed by this failure. He had a powerful ally in his appeal to the country's women: Eva Duarte, an attractive, shrewd and forceful young woman who had become Perón's mistress in 1944 when she was twenty-four years old, after liaisons with other powerful men. "Evita", as she was affectionately called, came from a lower-class background and was a clever judge of popular sentiment. She built her own network of influence even before she married Perón in late 1945.[14]

On a list of anti-Perón suffragists published by La Nación were not only the usual familiar names — Grierson, Chertkoff, Moreau, Rawson, Ocampo — but surnames of the oligarchy: Anchorena, Casares, Martínez and Pueyrredón. Perón's mobilization of working-class women had brought the elite philanthropists and the middle-class professional women together in a way that had been impossible for the past fifty years. As a more or less last-ditch attempt to counter Juan and Eva Perón's popularity with women, the National Assembly of Women was formed, including not only virtually all the feminist organizations but also the traditional social educational groups which favored suffrage, but not Perón's suffrage.[15] Also opposed to Perón was the Woman's Center for Civic Culture, a group of Catholic women, mostly upper class, which had been formed to help educate women to their civic responsibilities against the day when they would receive the vote. The Center's principal spokeswoman was Angelica Fuselli, a prominent Catholic social worker and philanthropist who represented Argentina on the Inter-American Commission on Women until she was removed by Perón in 1946. He closed the Center itself in 1949.[16]

Only Carmela Horne de Burmeister supported Perón's suffrage plan. She was not a Peronist, but she had always been more single-minded about suffrage than other Argentine feminists. In 1946 she gathered 170,000 names on a petition which she presented to the Congress. She was not concerned about suffrage by decrees, so long as women received the vote.[17]

In 1946, despite the opposition of all the national political parties, Juan Perón was elected president of the Republic of Argentina with fifty-four percent of the vote, in what was probably the most honest election in Argentine history. The Democratic Union, a coalition of parties formed to defeat Perón, had run José Tamborini, a lacklustre candidate who was nevertheless favored to win because of his strong support by traditional politicians, all of whom, along with the feminists, underestimated Perón's mass appeal.[18]

Perón gave his wife Eva the important public relations job of evangelist for women's rights in his new regime. After he had been in office a few months he and Eva presented a woman suffrage bill to Congress with a request that it be passed speedily by both houses. The feminist campaigns against him had had no impact; the lengthy speeches and debates in the Chamber were only a formality, because Perón clearly had the votes to pass the bill. Eva Perón had organized suffrage rallies, at which she gave long, dramatic speeches about the necessity of incorporating women into Argentine society. She gave regularly scheduled talks on the radio and delivered emotional speeches demanding that Congress give women their due. She promised men that, after enfranchisement, women would not become masculine or overbearing. In fact, she said, the right to political participation would make women more feminine and attractive; they would be Peronist partners to their men. Patriotic Argentine women would place God, country and Perón above their individual desires. And poor women, she promised, would no longer suffer from hopeless deprivation and humiliation in an unjust society dominated by the oligarchy.[19]

In spite of all this, a few conservatives tried to block the suffrage law, as they had so many times in the past. A group of Senators said they would like to test the interest in suffrage of women in various parts of the country; this tactic was abandoned when the galleries and even the Senate floor exploded into uproarious laughter at the suggestion.[20]

On 27 September, 1947, Argentine women were at last granted the right to vote. Thousands of female Peronists filled the streets of downtown Buenos Aires in celebration. Ironically, no members of the feminist movement were among the celebrants, with the possible exception of Carmela Horne de Burmeister and her followers.

The feelings of the feminists may be imagined. They had been rejected finally by the mass of women. After fifty years of pleading and exhortation, the working-class women of Argentina had chosen to follow a demagogue. And as if that were not bad enough, Eva Perón, ruthless and clever, had captured the imaginations of these women as no other woman had been able to do.[21] In 1977 Alicia Moreau spoke of the tragedy that "politically unclear women" had helped to bring upon the country. She dwelt on the crudities of Perón's regime: the intimidation, persecution and imprisonment. Victoria Ocampo, for instance, had been imprisoned for days with criminals and prostitutes; even upper-class women who criticized the government were not spared this sort of treatment. The feminists' attempt to stop the franchise, Dr Moreau said, was only "symbolic". She acknowledged that they had overemphasized the power of the female vote to effect social change and thus probably frightened people off.[22]

There is no question that the feminists had not grasped the realities of the political situation in 1946, or possibly at any time. There was no evidence of significant public support for Socialism, to which mast most feminists had nailed their flag. The women refused to face the fact that, for better or for worse, Juan and Eva Perón represented the aspirations of working-class people and appeared to women to be sincerely determined to improve their lives and working conditions and, most important, to have the real ability to make these improvements. It was not until Perón took office that most women had any real hope of a decent education and economic security for themselves and their daughters.

In 1949 Perón revised the Constitution of 1853. His Justicialista Constitution widened the powers of the president and the number of terms he could serve; it instituted a direct vote for president and senators, and extended the terms of deputies from four to six years. It put strong emphasis on state or corporate rights as opposed to individual rights. On a theoretical level, at least, it gave women legal equality in marriage with men, granting them equal control of their children with their husbands in case of marital separation. Although this Constitution was rescinded when Perón was ousted in 1955, on balance the legal position of women was improved because of these civil reforms.[23]

Juan Perón exerted power through his Peronista party and, after 1949, its Women's Branch (*Rama Femenina*) run by Eva Perón, who recruited old friends and acquaintances and members of the bureaucracy for her party; she asked only for unquestioning loyalty to Juan Perón and the New Argentina. Her party was "an astonishing success . . . It was [Eva's] first specifically political post and it constituted a recognition of her power in Argentina . . . By 1942 it had 500,000 members and 3,600 headquarters . . . It performed prodigies of organization. But it remained subordinate to Perón's wishes and its organization was stiflingly hierarchical."[24] Part of its success lay in the power of Eva's party to deliver concrete benefits and political power to its own community bureaucracy, and to working-class women, as well, who went to the neighborhood branches of the party (*unidades basicas*) to ask for money, political favors, or even educational opportunities for their children. Generally an attempt was made to respond to these requests. A corps of about thirty women worked directly under Eva Perón and could therefore advance in local and national politics, something that had been impossible before Perón. The Socialists had offered women freedom in the party, but few women were interested in the Socialist party. The Radicals had given only lip service to the rights of women.

Eva herself made the most of her humble origins, and even her illegitimate birth; the implication was that even the most downtrodden woman could have the opportunity in life to own fur coats and jewels, as long as she did not forget those who had stayed behind. Evita was a woman of the people who had power and flaunted it in the face of the oligarchy; working-class women felt she was speaking and acting for them. But there were more concrete advantages for working women in the Perón regime: piecework was declared illegal, and women's working hours were limited to forty-four a week. Minimum wage scales were instituted for women who did their employers' work at home. Eva Perón suggested a government subsidy for mothers based on the number of children, but this was not instituted.

So the protective legislation that the leaders of the old feminist movement and the Socialists had struggled for was finally implemented by the Peronistas, who also made an attempt to narrow the gap between men's and women's wages. Even minor improvements were eagerly appreciated by women frustrated by ineffectual union leadership which never made good its promises. The deep appeal of Peronism to the masses lay in its real ability to improve economic conditions and to articulate the people's passionate hatred and resentment of the oligarchy which they believed had always exploited them.

Eva Perón devoted much of her short political life to a vendetta against the Argentine elites. One of the most memorable episodes involved the Beneficent Society, which traditionally awarded an honorary presidency to the wife of the president of the Republic. In June, 1945, this honor was denied Eva Perón; the reason given was that she was too young and lacked philanthropic experience. Everyone knew that the real reasons for this snub were Evita's illegitimate birth, her seamy background and her position in a crude, brash government. Eva responded with sarcasm: perhaps the ladies would like to confer the presidency on her mother, whose age and experience might be more to their taste? The Society added further insult by offering the President's wife the opportunity to help with fund-raising events like canasta and bridge tournaments.

The Peróns' answer was swift and savage. Social justice, Eva Perón said, would replace charity in the New Argentina. The Beneficent Society was shut down by the government, which took over its building and installed a new agency there called the Foundation for Social Assistance and run by the President's wife, who ruthlessly dispensed with the services of any of the Society's remaining workers. Two years later, in June of 1948, the name of the Foundation was changed to the Eva Perón Foundation. It was no longer charity that was dispensed in the Society's quarters, but social aid, the rightful fulfillment of the nation's obligation toward those underprivileged who appreciated the efforts made on their behalf by Juan and Eva Perón.[25]

Under both its names, the Foundation, heavily subsidized by the state, supplied money for clinics, hospitals and dispensing pharmacies, gave away food and clothing at regular intervals, dramatically expanded the number of hospital beds in the country and provided disaster relief both in and outside of Argentina. And it increased by one quarter the number of schools. Quite naturally, a heavy barrage of propaganda accompanied these accomplishments. Eva was given impressive titles by the press, like "The Lady of Hope".[26]

The Women's Party had an electric effect on the election of 1951. Perón's vote grew from 1.4 million or fifty-four percent in 1946 to 4.6 million or sixty-four percent in 1951. Peronistas took every Senate seat and nine out of ten seats in the Chamber of Deputies. Over ninety percent of the eligible women voted, with Perón's share of their vote running between fifty-three and eighty-three percent.[27] Seven women senators and twenty-four women deputies were elected, all Peronistas. Several female candidates who ran as Socialists and Communists were defeated. In 1953 a Peronist woman, Delia de Parodi, was elected vice president of the Chamber of Deputies. Eva herself had intended to be the candidate for vice president in 1951, but the army would not allow it. There was a deep suspicion, for one thing, that funds from her Foundation were going into the Peróns' private pocket. Accordingly Juan Perón withdrew her name from consideration; she was in any case too ill to make a strong protest. She gave speeches in which she said she had no desire for political office; she wanted only to serve Perón as his wife, and the country as the head of the Foundation and the Women's Party.

The election of 1951 was riddled with intimidation and corruption. Perón used his considerable power over the press and the unions to win, although economic conditions were not good and there were growing signs of discontent. After the election the government clamped down harshly on its enemies with censorship and travel bans.

Nineteen-fifty-two was a disastrous year economically, but the greatest disaster for Perón was the death of Eva from cancer at age thirty-three. She had continued her effusive praise of Perón almost to the day of her death. Her husband attempted to extend the considerable mystique which had surrounded her: "The Lady of Hope" became "The Martyr of the Descamisados". But Perón went too far when he attempted to have her canonized. The Church was outraged. It had supported him in 1946 and he had shown his appreciation by making religious instruction mandatory in the schools and giving government subsidies to private Church schools. In his anger at the Church's refusal to bestow sainthood on his wife, and its reluctance to give him further support, the President annulled the religious instruction law, rescinded the subsidies for Church schools and announced pending legislation to legalize divorce and prostitution. The Church's response was predictable. Perón had never been really trusted and now stories circulated about his liaisons with teenaged girls since Eva's death. The Church banded with the army against Perón and its strength was unassailable, especially at a time of general economic discontent. By March, 1955, the situation had deteriorated to the point that the government had firm plans to separate church and state, and priests were being arrested. Here the army stepped in and Perón was forced to resign.[28]

He had put a fragile coalition together by the strength of

his personality; he had no coherent political philosophy. Robert J. Alexander has said that Perón's support, in his heyday which ran from 1945 to 1949, came from a loose "coalition of the dominant portion of the military . . . the Church, the new industrialists, a small portion of the middle class, the old urban industrial class, and the recently urbanized migrants from the interior. Beyond a concern for industrialization, the creation of a high consumption economy and the safeguarding of the national patrimony, these groups had little in common."[29] When they began to unravel, it was over for Perón.

In the same way, Eva Perón had no real feminist philosophy. She spoke contemptuously of committed feminists as masculine women of the oligarchy, castrating women who wanted to be men, false progressives who copied foreign ideas, snobs and cultural imperialists, anti-nationalist and therefore anti-Perón. She held the nineteenth-century idea that women could improve society by civilizing and humanizing men; at the same time she credited Perón with having educated her about the need for women's rights. The woman's movement, she said, could accomplish great things only if it was associated with a great man: she herself was motivated not by reason, but by her heart and her heart belonged to Perón. She was the student, he the teacher; he provided reason, she emotion. It was the historic role of women to follow great men and when Perón told her that women should have their rights, she believed him because he was a genius. Personal loyalty to Perón was, she said, synonymous with the woman's movement. "For a woman to be a Peronist," she said, "is before anything to be loyal to Perón, subordinate to Perón, and to have blind confidence in Perón."[30] At the same time she insisted that women were as capable as men of making political decisions.[31]

In contrast to the Spartan appearance of the early feminists, Eva Perón dyed her hair and wore jewelry and expensive clothes. Among working women she inspired not envy but admiration. She made it a rule that the women working in her political organizations should be as chic and "feminine" as possible. In the textbooks and histories that proliferated in Argentina after 1946, the leaders of the old feminist movement — particularly Cecilia Grierson and Alicia Moreau de Justo — are treated as well-meaning but politically naïve women who, because of their narrow ideologies and attachment to European ideas, were incapable of understanding the greatness of Perón.[32]

In 1963, when Perón had been in exile for eight years, the liberal and Socialist feminists announced that the woman suffrage bill had been passed by the Argentine Congress in response to the demands of the Pan-American Union's Inter-American Commission for Women, and not because of Juan and Eva Perón. Even after a decade and a half, the feminists could not accept their own inability to reach the majority of Argentine women. It was true that the Pan-American Union had tried to put pressure on Argentina, as well as on other Latin American countries, to give women the vote. Perón may have noted this, and certainly he and his wife were aware of the international trend toward increased rights for women which had begun after the first World War. The Church itself had supported woman suffrage after World War II. But it was Juan Perón who, motivated basically by the desire to build a loyal constituency of women to protect his political base, made suffrage possible and included it in his revised Constitution of 1949.

Women have never since had as large a representation in Argentine government as they had under Perón, but they had been brought by him into the political system and many of his reforms remain in place. The feminists' vocal anti-Peronism was out of step with the feelings of the mass of their countrymen. From 1955 to 1958 two Argentine presidents attempted campaigns called "Peronism without Perón". These were not successful. Certainly working-class women were loyal to Perón long after he was deposed. In subsequent elections at least through 1965 women's voting patterns did not vary significantly from men's.[33]

In 1977 Dr Moreau de Justo admitted that she and her colleagues had never grasped the significance of nationalism to the Argentine people. They had railed against the *caudillo* tradition without understanding the importance of that tradition to the masses, who had historically responded to any strong leader who offered them an escape from the country's rigid class system. On the other hand, Dr Moreau said that Perón was the greatest disaster for Argentina in the twentieth century. She chose not to discuss the feminist movement in terms of success or failure. It was, she said, one of a series of events in the struggle for democracy and social justice in Argentina. Its failure, she said, is not important. What is important is the ideal itself: a vision of a free, democratic Argentina in which women have been able to achieve true equality.

Notes

[1] Eva Duarte Perón, *Evita By Evita* (NY: Proteus Books, 1953), p. 180.

[2] Among the many accounts of the political situation in the era immediately preceding Perón are: Rbt. J. Alexander, *The Perón Era* (NY: Russell and Russell, 1965): Baily, *Labor, Nationalism and Politics*; Barager, *Why Perón Came to Power*; Falcoff and Dolkhart, eds., *Argentina in Depression*; Goldwert, *Democracy, Militarism and Nationalism*; Ruth and Leonard Greenup, *Revolution Before Breakfast, 1941-46* (Chapel Hill: U of N. Car. Press, 1947); Ray Josephs, *Argentine Diary: The Inside Story of the Coming of Fascism* (NY: Random House, 1944); Joseph Page, *Perón, A Biography* (NY: Random House, 1983); Marta Panaia, Ricardo Lesser, Pedro Skupch, *Estudios sobre los orígenes del Peronismo II* (BA: Siglo XXI Argentina, 1973), 5-21.; Rbt. A. Potash, *The Army and Politics in Argentina, 1928-1945: Yrigoyen to Perón* (Stanford U. Press, 1969); Edmund Oscar Smith, "Argentina and the Problem of Hemispheric Solidarity" Diss. Univ. of Chgo., 1950.

[3] *La Prensa*, 11 Dec., 1943.

[4] Josephs. pp. 5-116.

[5] Hollander, p. 250.

[6] *El Porvenir*, 28 Nov., 1942. See this newspaper for 1941-1942. Also *El Pampero 1942-1943*.

[7] Marysa Gerassi, "Argentine Nationalism of the Right" Diss. Columbia Univ., 1964, pp. 113-181.

[8] Rock, *Argentina 1516-1982*, pp. 253-258.

[9] Lucila de Gregorio Lavié, *Trajectoría de la condición social de las mujeres Argentinas* (Santa Fe: Univ. del Littoral, 1947), 17.

[10] Rock, p. 259.

[11] Justa de Salazar Pringles, "La mujer Argentina ante el sufragio" in *Anuario Socialista* (1946), p. 169.

[12] Eugenia Silveyra de Oyuela, "No queremos votar!" in *La Nación*, 12 July, 1945.

[13] Josefina Marpons, *La mujer y su lucha con el ambiente* (BA: El Ateneo, 1947), p. 94.

[14] Moreau de Justo, *Como votar?*, p. 6.

[15] For information on Eva Perón see Benigno Acossano, *Eva Perón: su verdadera vida* (BA: Editorial Lanus, 1955); Sharon Akridge, "Cinderella from the Pampas: María Eva Duarte Perón, Argentine First Lady 1919-1952" Diss. Univ. of California, 1976; Anzoátegui, *La mujer y la historia*; Antonio Benedetti, *Perón y Eva: trajectoría y fin de un regimen* (Mexico City: Editores Panamericanos Asociados, 1956);

María Flores, *The Woman with the Whip: Eva Perón* (Garden City: Doubleday, 1952); Nicholas Fraser and Marysa Navarro, *Eva Perón* (NY: Norton, 1980); Hollander, "Women in the Political Economy of Argentina"; de Lavié, *La ciudadana*; Meyer, *Victoria Ocampo*; Eva Perón, *La razón de mi vida* (BA: Editorial Peuser, 1951); E. F. Sánchez Zinny, *El culto de la infamia: historia documentada de la segunda tiranía Argentina* (BA: n.p., 1958); Juan José Sebreli, *Eva Perón, adventura o militante?* (BA: Ediciones Siglo Veinte, 1966); J. M. Taylor, *Eva Perón: The Myths of a Woman* (Chicago: Univ. of Chicago, 1979).

[16]*La Nación*, 7 July, 1945.

[17]Files of the Centro Femenino de Cultura Cívica, BA; Blanca Cassagne Seres, *Debe votar la mujer?* (BA: Editorial Licurgo, 1946); Celina Arenza, *Sin Memoria* (BA: Pellegrini, 1980), pp. 32-33.

[18]Sosa de Newton, *Diccionario*, pp. 176-177.

[19]Page, pp. 139-140.

[20]See *La Nación*, 20 March, 1947; *La Razón*, 22 Sept., 1947.

[21]*La Nación*, 5-11 Sept., 1947.

[22]See *El Hogar*, 8 Nov., 1945; *La Nación*, 23 Sept., 1972.

[23]Author's interview with Alicia Moreau de Justo, 1 Aug., 1977. See also Meyer, *Victoria Ocampo*, pp. 152-159.

[24]Interview 1 Aug., 1977.

[25]Fraser and Navarro, pp. 107-108.

[26]*Ibid*, p. 116.

[27]Rock, p. 307.

[28]*Ibid*, pp. 314-315.

[29]Alexander, *The Perón Era*, p. 62.

[30]Taylor, p. 76; *La Nación*, 24 Sept., 1947.

[31]*Dinamis*, July, 1969.

[32]See Eva Perón, *La razón de mi vida*.

[33]See Anzoátegui and de Lavié; Paul H. Lewis, "The Female Vote in Argentina, 1958-1965" in *Comparative Politics* Vol. 3, No. 4 (Jan., 1971), 428.

Bibliography

Books

Alba, Victor. *Politics and the Labor Movement in Latin America.* Stanford: Stanford University Press, 1968.

Album biográfico de los Librepensadores de la República Argentina. Buenos Aires: Otto Rossaly, 1910.

Alexander, Robert. *Organized Labor in Latin America.* New York: Free Press, 1965.
_____. *Juan Domingo Perón: A History.* Boulder: Westview Press, 1979.
_____. *The Perón Era.* New York: Russell and Russell, 1965.

Andrews, George Reid. *The Afro-Argentines of Buenos Aires, 1800-1900.* Madison: The University of Wisconsin Press, 1980.

Anzoátegui, Yderla G. *La mujer y la historia del feminismo mundial.* Buenos Aires: n.p., 1953.

Arenza, Celina. *Sin memoria.* Buenos Aires: Pellegrini, 1980.

Avrich, Paul. *An American Anarchist: The Life of Voltairine le Cleyre.* Princeton: Princeton University Press, 1978.

Bailey, Samuel. *Labor, Nationalism, and Politics in Argentina.* New Brunswick: Rutgers University Press, 1967.

Barager, Joseph. *Why Perón Came to Power.* New Brunswick: Rutgers University Press, 1967.

Belloni, Albert. *Del anarquismo al Peronismo.* Buenos Aires: A. Peña Gillo, 1960.

Bialet-Massé. *El estado de las clases obreras Argentinas a comienzos del siglo.* 2nd ed. Córdoba: Universidad Nacional de Cordoba, 1968.

Blachman, Morris J. *Eve in an Adamocracy: The Politics of Women in Brazil.* New York: New York University, 1977.

Boxer, Charles. *Women in Iberian Expansion Overseas, 1415-1815.* New York: Oxford University Press, 1975.

Bravo, Mario. *Derechos civiles de la mujer.* Buenos Aires: n.p., 1932.

Bourne, Richard. *Political Leaders of Latin America.* New York: Knopf, 1970.

Brumana, Herminia. *Cartas a las mujeres Argentinas*. Santiago: Ercilla, 1936.

Bunge, Octavio. *Obras Completas de Octavio Bunge*. Vol. 3. Madrid: n.p. 1928.

Bunge de Gálvez, Delfina. *Las mujeres y la vocación*. Buenos Aires: Editorial Poblet, 1922.

Burns, E. Bradford. *The Poverty of Progress: Latin America in the Nineteenth Century*. Berkeley: University of California, 1980.

Caroche, Pedro. *Nuestra Asociación*. Buenos Aires: La asociación Unión Normalista de Mercedes, 1889.

Cassagne Serres, Blanca. *¿Debe votar la mujer?* Buenos Aires: Editorial Licurgo, 1946.

del Castillo. Bernal Díaz. *The Discovery and Conquest of Mexico, 1517-1521*. Introduction by Irving A. Leonard. New York: Farrar, Straus and Cudahy, 1956.

Cocca, Aldo Armando. *Ley de sufragio femenino*. Buenos Aires: El Ateneo, 1948.

Colmo, Alfredo. *Derechos civiles de la mujer ante la experiencia*. Buenos Aires: Taleres Gráficos Tudor, 1929.

Consejo Nacional de Mujeres de la República Argentina. *Historia de la Biblioteca del Consejo Nacional de Mujeres*. Buenos Aires: Gráfico "Oceana," 1936.

Cordasco, Francesco and Pitkin, Thomas Monroe. *The White Slave Trade and the Immigrants*. 2nd. ed. Detroit: Blaine Etheridge, 1981.

Crowley, Francis G. *Sarmiento, Teacher of the Americas*. New York: Twayne Publishers, 1972.

Dellepiane, Antonio. *El testamento de Rosas, la hija del dictador*. Buenos Aires: Editorial Oberón, 1957.

Deutsch, Sandra F. McGee. *Counterrevolution in Argentina, 1900-1932: The Argentine Patriotic League*. Lincoln: University of Nebraska, 1986.

Dickman, Enrique. *Recuerdos de un militante socialista*. Buenos Aires: La Vanguardia, 1949.

Dreier, Katharine. *Five Months in the Argentine from a Woman's Point of View*. NY: Frederick Fairchild Sherman, 1920.

Evans, Richard. *The Feminists*. New York: Barnes and Noble, 1977.

Falcoff, Mark and Dolkhart, Donald H. eds. *Prologue to Perón, Argentina in Depression and War, 1930-1943*. Berkeley: University of California Press, 1975.

Flexnor, Eleanor. *Century of Struggle: The Women's Rights Movement in the United States.*

Flores, María. *The Woman With the Whip: Eva Perón.* Garden City: Doubleday, 1952.

Fraser, Nicholas and Marysa Navarro. *Eva Perón.* New York: Norton, 1980.

Fuselli, Angelica. *El voto de la mujer Argentina.* Buenos Aires: Comisión Interamericana de Mujeres, 1945.
_____ . *A las mujeres de mi país.* Buenos Aires: Comisión Interamericana de Mujeres, 1945.

Gibson, Charles. *Spain in America.* New York: Harper and Row, 1966.

Goldwert, Marvin. *Democracy, Militarism, and Nationalism in Argentina, 1930-1966: An Interpretation.* Austin: University of Texas Press, 1972.

Graham, R. B. Cunninghame. *The Conquest of the River Plate.* New York: Greenwood Press, 1968.

Greenup, Ruth and Leonard. *Revolution Before Breakfast: Argentina, 1941-46.* Chapel Hill: The University of North Carolina Press, 1947.

Gregorio Lavié, Lucila. *La Ciudadana, para las mujeres que votan.* Buenos Aires: Libro de Edición Argentina, 1948.
_____ . *Trajectoria de la condición social de las mujeres Argentinas.* Santa Fe: Universidad Nacional del Litoral, 1947.

Grierson, Cecilia. *La decadencia del Consejo Nacional de Mujeres de la República Argentina.* Buenos Aires: N.P. 1910.

Gunther, John. *Inside South America.* New York: Harper and Row, 1966.

Hahner, June. *Women in Latin American History: Their Lives and Views.* Los Angeles: UCLA Latin American Center Publications, 1976.

Henderson, James D. and Linda Roddy. *Ten Notable Women of Latin America.* Chicago: Nelson-Hall, 1978.

Herring, Hubert. *A History of Latin America.* New York: Knopf, 1968.

Hobsbawm, Eric. *Primitive Rebels.* New York: Norton, 1959.

Horne de Burmeister, Carmela. *Asociación Argentina del Sufragio Femenino: fines y propósitos de los estatutos.* Buenos Aires: n.p., 1932.
_____ . *Como se organizó en la Argentina el movimiento en favor de los derechos politicos de la mujer por el Comité Argentina Pro-voto de la Mujer, hoy, Asociación Argentina del Sufragio Femenino.* Buenos Aires: Ricra y Cia., 1933.

Howard, Jennie E. *In Distant Climes and Other Years.* Buenos Aires: American Press, 1931.

Imaz, Luis de. *Los Que Mandan*. Translated by C. A. Astiz. Albany: State University of New York Press, 1970.

International Council of Women, *Our Common Cause*. New York: National Council of Women of the United States, 1933.

International Survey Committee. *International Survey of the Young Men's and Young Women's Christian Associations*. New York: n.p., 1932.

Janik, Allan and Toulmin, Stephan. *Wittgenstein's Vienna*. New York: Simon and Schuster, 1973.

Joll, James. *The Anarchists*. Boston: Little, Brown and Co., 1964.

Josephs, Ray. *Argentine Diary*. London: Victor Gollancz Ltd., 1945.

Justo, Juan B. *Socialismo*. Buenos Aires: La Vanguardia, 1920.

Justo, Sara. *El movimiento femenino en Europa*. Buenos Aires: Gráfico Collins, 1909.

Kaplan, Marion K. *The Jewish Feminist Movement in Germany: The Campaigns of the Judischer Frauenbund, 1904-1928*. Westport, Conn.: Greenwood Press, 1979.

Kaplan, Temma. *Anarchists of Andalusia*. Princeton: Princeton University Press, 1977.

Korn, Alejandro. *Influencias filosóficas en la evolución nacional*. Buenos Aires: Claridad, n.d.

Lanteri, Julieta. *Contribución al estudio del deciduoma maligno*. Buenos Aires: Nicolás Marona, 1906.
_____ . *La mujer librepensadora*. Buenos Aires: n.p., 1909.

La Palma de Emery, Celia. *Acción pública y privada en favor de la mujer y del niño*. Buenos Aires: Alfa y Omega, 1910.

Larraya, Antonio Pagés. *Gabriela de Coni y sus precursoras*. Buenos Aires: Ediciones Culturales Argentinas, 1965.

Lavrin, Asunción. ed. *Latin American Women: Historical Perspectives*. Westport, Conn.: Greenwood Press, 1978.

Liss, Sheldon B. *Marxist Thought in Latin America*. Berkeley: University of California Press, 1984.

Lockhart, James. *Spanish Peru 1532-1560, A Colonial Society*. Madison: The University of Wisconsin Press, 1968.

Lombroso, Gina. *The Soul of Woman: Reflections on Life*. New York: Dutton, 1910.

Loncarina, Alfredo G. Kohn. *Cecilia Grierson: Vida y obra de la primera médica Argentina*. Buenos Aires: Editorial Stilcograf, 1976.

Longhi, Luis R. *Sufragio Femenino*. Buenos Aires: Baiocco, 1932.

Luiggi, Alice Houston. *Sixty-Five Valiants*. Gainesville: University of Florida Press, 1965.

Luisi, Paulina. *La mujer en la democracia*. Buenos Aires: La Union Argentina de Mujeres, 1932.

Lynch, John. *Argentine Dictator, Juan Manuel de Rosas, 1829-1852*. New York: Oxford University Press, 1981.
———. *The Spanish-American Revolutions, 1808-1826*. New York: W. W. Norton and Company, 1973.

Madrid Páez, S. *Sociedad de Beneficencia de la capital; Su misión y sus obras*. Buenos Aires: Talleres Gráficos de Huérfanos, 1923.

Mafud, Julio. *La revolución sexual Argentina*. Buenos Aires: Editorial Américalee, 1971.

Mandelbaum, Maurice. *History, Man, and Reason: A Study in Nineteenth Century Thought*. Baltimore: Johns Hopkins Press, 1971.

Marotta, Sebastián. *El movimiento sindical Argentino: Su génesis y desarollo, 1857-1914*. Buenos Aires: Ediciones Libera, 1960.

Marpons, Josefina. *La mujer y su lucha con el ambiente*. Buenos Aires: El Ateneo, 1947.

McDonald, Austin F. *Government of the Argentine Republic*. New York: Thomas Y. Crowell, 1942.

McGann, Thomas. *Argentina, The United States and the Inter-american System, 1880-1914*. Cambridge: Harvard University Press, 1968.

Meyer, Doris. *Victoria Ocampo, Against the Tide*. New York: George Braziller, 1979.

Millet, Kate. *Sexual Politics*. New York: Vintage, 1973.

Molina, Enrique. *Una sombra donde sueña, Camila O'Gorman*. Buenos Aires: Corregidor, 1984.

Moreau de Justo, Alicia. *Como votar? Para que votar?* Buenos Aires: Unión de Mujeres Socialistas, 1949.
———. *La emancipación civil de la mujer*. Buenos Aires: Union Feminista Nacional, 1919.
———. *El feminismo el la evolución social*. Buenos Aires: Ateneo Popular, 1911.
———. *La mujer en la democracia*. Buenos Aires: El Ateneo, 1945.
———. *El socialismo de Juan B. Justo*. Buenos Aires: Editorial Polis, 1946.
———. *Socialismo y la mujer*. Buenos Aires: Editorial La Vanguardia, 1946.

Mörner, Magnus. *Race Mixture in the History of Latin America*. Boston: Little, Brown and Company, 1967.

National Council of Women of the United States. *The Evolution of the*

International Council of Women: Part I, 1888-1913. New York: 1956.

Naipaul, V.S. *The Return of Eva Perón*. New York: Knopf, 1980.

Ocampo, Victoria. *La mujer y su expresión*. Buenos Aires: Sur, 1936.
————. *Testimonios I*. Madrid: Revista del Occidente, 1935.
————. *Testimonios II*. Buenos Aires: Sur, 1941.

Oddone, Jacinto. *Declaración de principios y programa del partido socialista*. Buenos Aires: Partido Socialista Democrática, 1972.

O'Neill, William. *Everyone Was Brave: A History of Feminism in America*. Chicago: Quadrangle, 1971.

Ortiz, Raúl Scalabrini. *Política Británica en el Río de la Plata*. Buenos Aires: Editorial Reconquista, 1940.

Page, Joseph. *Perón*. New York: Random House, 1983.

Palacios, Alfredo. *Legislación del trabajo, de mujeres y niños*. Buenos Aires: Imprento Progreso, 1908.

Panaia, Marta, Ricardo Lesser and Pedro Skupch. eds. *Estudios sobre los orígenes del Peronismo*. Buenos Aires: Siglo XXI Argentina, 1973.

Parker, William B. *Argentines of Today*. Buenos Aires: Hispanic Society of America, 1920.

Paulson, Ross Evans. *Women's Suffrage and Prohibition: A Comparative Study of Equality and Social Control*. Glenview, Ill.: Scott Foresman, 1973.

Perón, Eva. *Historia del Peronismo*. Buenos Aires: Escuela Superior Peronista, 1951.
————. *La mujer puede y debe votar*. Buenos Aires: n.p. 1951.
————. *La razón de mi vida*. Buenos Aires: Editorial Peuser, 1951.

Pescatello, Ann. ed. *Female and Male in Latin America*. Pittsburgh: University of Pittsburgh Press, 1973.
————. *The Female in Iberian Families, Societies and Cultures*. Westport, Conn.: Greenwood Press, 1973.

Phillips, Rachel. *Alfonsina Storni: From Poetess to Poet*. London: Tamesis Books Limited, 1975.

Picón-Salas, Mariano. *A Cultural History of Spanish America*. Berkeley: University of California Press, 1965.

Potash, Robert. *The Army and Politics in Argentina, 1928-1945: Yrigoyen to Perón*. Stanford: Stanford University Press, 1969.

Quataert, Jean. *Reluctant Feminists in German Social Democracy, 1885-1917*. Princeton: Princeton University Press, 1979.

Quesada, Ernesto. *La question femenina*. Buenos Aires: Pablo E. Coni, 1899.

Ramos, Jorge Abelardo. *Historia de la nación Latinomericana.* Buenos Aires: A. Pena Lillo, 1973.

Rawson, Elvira. *Apuntes sobre higiene de la mujer.* Buenos Aires: n.p., 1892.

Repetto, Nicolás. *Mis Noventa Años.* Buenos Aires: Bases, 1962.

Reusmann de Battola, Elvira. *El libro de oro de la mujer Americana.* Buenos Aires: A. de Martino, 1910.

Rex, Crawford Williams. *A Century of Latin American Thought.* Cambridge: Harvard University Press, 1944.

Rock, David. *Argentina 1516-1982, From Spanish Colonization to the Falklands War.* Berkeley: University of California Press, 1985.
_____ *Politics in Argentina, 1890-1930: The Rise and Fall of Radicalism.* London: n.p., 1975.

Romero, Jose Luis. *A History of Argentine Political Thought.* Translated by Thomas F. McGann. Stanford: Stanford University Press, 1984.

Rondanina, Esteban F. *Liberalismo, masonería y socialismo en la evolución nacional.* Buenos Aires: Ediciones Libera, 1965.

Rothman, Sheila. *Woman's Proper Place: A History of Changing Ideals and Practices, 1870 to the Present.* New York: Basic Books, 1978.

Rouco Buela, Juana. *Historia de un ideal vivido por una mujer.* Buenos Aires: Julio Kaufman, 1964.

Sarmiento, Domingo F. *Life in the Argentine Republic in the Days of the Tyrants; or Civilization and Barbarism.* New York: Hafner Publishing Corp. 1971.
_____ . *Páginas confidenciales: Sus luchas, sus pasiones, sus truinfos, las mujeres en su vida.* Buenos Aires: Editorial Elevación, 1944.

Schultz de Mantovani, Freyda. *La mujer en la vida nacional.* Buenos Aires: Galetea Nueva Vision, 1960.

Scobie, James R. *Argentina: A City and a Nation.* New York: Oxford University Press, 1971.
_____ . *Buenos Aires: Plaza to Suburb, 1870-1910.* New York: Oxford University Press, 1974.

Shulman, Alix Kates. *Red Emma Speaks: Selected Writings and Speeches by Emma Goldman.* New York: Vintage, 1972.

Sklar, Kathryn Kish. *Catharine Beecher: A Study in American Domesticity.* New York: Norton, 1973.

Smith, Peter. *Argentina and the Failure of Democracy: Conflict Among Political Elites: 1904-1955.* Madison: University of Wisconsin Press, 1974.
_____ . *Politics and Beef in Argentina: Patterns of Conflict and Change.* New York: Columbia University Press, 1969.

Solari, Manuel Horacio. *Historia de la educación Argentina.* Buenos Aires: Editorial Paidos, 1972.

Solberg, Carl. *Immigration and Nationalism: Argentina and Chile, 1890-1914*. Austin: University of Texas Press, 1970.

Spalding, Hobart. *La clase trabajadora Argentina: Documentos para su historia, 1890-1912*. Buenos Aires: Editorial Galerna, 1970.

Sosa de Newton, Lily. *Las Argentinas de ayer y hoy*. Buenos Aires: Editorial L. V. Zanetti, 1967.
_____ . *Diccionario biográfico de mujeres Arentinas*. Buenos Aires: Artes Gráficas Chiesino, 1972.

Snow, Peter. *Argentine Radicalism: The History and Doctrine of the Radical Civic Union*. Iowa City: The University of Iowa Press, 1965.

Stein, Stanley J. and Barbara H. Stein. *The Colonial Legacy of Latin America*. New York: Oxford University Press, 1970.

Stites, Richard. *The Women's Liberation Movement in Russia: Feminism, Nihilism, and Bolshevism*. Princeton: Princeton University Press, 1978.

Szuchman, Mark. *Mobility and Integration in Urban Argentina: Córdoba in the Liberal Era*. Austin: University of Texas Press, 1980.

Taylor, J. M. *Eva Perón: The Myths of a Woman*. Chicago: University of Chicago Press, 1979.

Teggart, Frederick J. *Theory and Practice of History*. 2nd ed. Berkeley: University of California Press, 1977.

Torres, José Luís. *La década infame, 1930-1940*. Buenos Aires: Editorial Freeland, 1973.

Vida de Grandes Argentinos. Buenos Aires: Fossati, 1960.

Weimann, Jeanne Madeline and Anita Miller. *The Fair Women: The Story of the Woman's Building, World's Columbian Exposition, Chicago, 1893*. Chicago: Academy Chicago Publishers, 1981.

Zea, Leopoldo. *The Latin-American Mind*. Norman: University of Oklahoma Press, 1963.

Articles

Alexander, Robert J. "The Latin American Labor Leader." In *Industrial Relations and Social Change in Latin America*. Edited by W. Form and A. Blum. Gainesville: University of Florida, 1965.

Berrando, María L. "Una semilla mas." In *La paz por la cultura*. Buenos Aires: La Vanguardia, 1936.

Brenzel, Barbara. "Lancaster Industrial School for Girls: A Social Portrait of a Nineteenth-Century Reform School for Girls."*Feminist Studies* 1, No. 2 (1975): 40-51.

Caras y Caretas. "El voto femenino." XXXII no. 1625 (November 23, 1929).

Coghlan, Eduardo. "La denatalidad en la Argentina." *Revista de Economía* (October 1945): 494-96; (December 1945): 577-81.

Conway, Jill. "Stereotypes of Femininity in a Theory of Sexual Evolution." In *Suffer and Be Still: Women in the Victorian Age.* Edited by Martha Vicinus. Bloomington: University of Indiana Press, 1973.

Corbiére, Emilio. "Alicia Moreau de Justo." *Revista LYRA*, Vol. 231 (1977).

Criterio. "La conferencia sobre la condición jurídica y social de la mujer casada." X: no. 497. (September 9, 1937).

DeGrand, Alexander. "Women Under Italian Fascism," *The Historical Journal* 19:4 (1976): 947-968.

Dinamis, "Eva Perón, mujer o mito." No. 10 (July, 1969).

DuBois, Ellen. "The Radicalism of the Woman Suffrage Movement: Notes Toward the Reconstruction of Nineteenth-Century Feminism." *Feminist Studies* 3, Nos. 1-2 (Fall, 1975): 63-71.

Etchepareborda, Roberto. "La Estructura Socio-Política Argentina y la Generación del Ochenta." *LARR* 13 (1978): 127-34.

Feijoó, María Carmen. "Las luchas feministas." *Todo es Historia* 11, No. 128 (January, 1978): 7-23.

Franceschi, Gustavo. "Ante derrumbo de la natalidad." *Criterio* XVI No. 789: 345-48.

Gage, Thomas. "Mexico City, 1635" in *Impressions of Latin America.* Edited by Frank MacShane. New York: William Morrow and Company, 1963.

Germani, Gino. "Mass Immigration and Modernization in Argentina." In *Masses in Latin America.* Edited by Irving Louis Horowitz. New York: Oxford University Press, 1970.

Gordon, Linda. Review of *The Politics of Domesticity: Women, Evangelism, and Temperance in Nineteenth-Century America,* by Barbara Leslie Epstein. Middletown: Wesleyan University Press, 1981. In *Signs* 7, No. 4 (1982): 892.

Guisti, Roberto. "Alfonsina." *Nosotros*, Vol. 3, No. 32 (1938).

Guy, Donna. "Women, Peonage, and Industrialization: Argentina, 1810-1914." *LARR* 16, No. 3 (1981), 81.

Hahner, June. "Feminism, Women's Rights and the Suffrage Movement in Brazil." *LARR* 15, No. 1 (1980), 65-112.

Hause, Steven C. and Anne K. Kenney. "The Limits of Suffragist Behavior: Legalism and Militancy in France, 1876-1922." *AHR* 86, No. 4 (October, 1981): 781-806.

Herrera, L. "Liceo nacional de señoritas de la Capital." *Boletín de Instrucción Pública* 12 (May, 1913): 89.

Hollander, Nancy. "Si Evita viviera." *Latin American Perspectives* I:3, 42-58.

Kaplan, Temma. "Female Consciousness and Collective Action: The Case of Barcelona, 1910-1918." *Signs* 73, No. 3 (Spring, 1982): 545-66.

Kelly-Gadol, Joan. "The Social Relation of the Sexes: Methodological Implications of Women's History." *Signs* 1, No. 4 (1976): 809-23.

Kenworthy, Elton. "The Function of the Little Known Case in Theory Formation on What Peronism Wasn't." *Comparative Politics* 6 (October, 1973): 17-43.

Larroca, Jorge. "Un anarchista en Buenos Aires." *Todo es Historia* 47 (March, 1971): 45-57.

Lattes, Zulma R. de. and C. Wainerman. "Empleo femenino y desarrollo económico." *Dessarrollo Economico* 17, No. 66 (July-September, 1977): 301-17.

Lavrin, Asunción. "Women in Convents: Their Economic and Social Role in Mexico." In *Liberating Women's History: Theoretical and Critical Essays*. Edited by Berenice Carroll. Urbana: University of Illinois Press, 1976.

Lawton, Henry. "The Myth of Altruism: A Psychohistory of Public Agency Social Work." *Journal of Psychohistory* 9, No. 3 (Winter, 1982): 265-308.

Lewis, Paul. "The Female Vote in Argentina, 1958-1965." *Comparative Politics* 3 (January 1971): 425-41.

Little, Cynthia Jeffress. "Moral Reform and Feminism: A Case Study." *Journal of Interamerican Studies and World Affairs* 17, no. 4 (1975): 386-97.

Lozada, Jorgelina. "Debe y quiere votar la mujer Argentina?" *La Novela Semanal* (March 3, 1936).

Luiggi, Alice Houston. "Some Letters of Sarmiento and Mary Mann," *HAHR*, (May, 1952): 187-212.

Moreau de Justo, Alicia. "Las mujeres y la paz." in *La paz por la cultura*. Buenos Aires: La Vanguardia, 1936.
_____ . "Participación de la mujer en la política nacional." *Revista de la Universidad de Córdoba* X No. 1-2 (Marzo-Junio, 1969): 283-304.

Ocampo, Victoria. "Virginia Woolf in my Mind." *Nimrod* (Spring-Summer, 1976): 142-150.

de Onis, Juan. "Isabelita's Terrible Legacy." *New York Times Magazine* (March 21, 1976).

Schipske, Evelyn. "An Analysis of the Consejo Nacional de Mujeres de

Peru." *Journal of Interamerican Studies and World Affairs* 17, no. 4 (1975): 526-38.

Smith, Hilda. "Feminism and the Methodology of Women's History." *Liberating Women's History: Theoretical and Critical Essays.* Edited by Berenice Carroll. Urbana: University of Illinois Press, 1976.

Smith-Rosenberg, Carroll. "The Hysterical Woman: Sex Roles and Role Conflict in Nineteenth-Century America." In *Ourselves/Our Past: Psychological Approaches to American History.* Edited by Robert J. Brugger. Baltimore: Johns Hopkins Press, 1981.

Smith, Peter. "The Social Base of Peronism." *HAHR* 52 (February, 1972): 55-73.

Soeiro, Susan. "The Social and Economic Role of the Convent: Women and Nuns in Colonial Bahia, 1670-1800." *HAHR* 54, No. 2 (1974): 209-32.

Stansell, Christine. "Women, Children, and the Uses of the Streets: Class and Gender Conflicts in New York City, 1850-1860." *Feminist Studies* 8, No. 2 (Summer, 1982): 309-36.

Vázquez, Juan Adolfo. "La filosofía en las universidades Argentinas." In *Antología filosofía Argentina del siglo XX.* Buenos Aires: University of Buenos Aires, 1965.

Williams, Margaret Todaro. "Psychoanalysis and Latin American History." In *New Approaches to Latin American History.* Edited by Richard Graham and Peter H. Smith. Austin: University of Texas Press, 1974.

Other Works

Actas de la Sociedad de Beneficencia, 1823-1946. Buenos Aires: In the Archivo General de la Nación.

Archivo de *La Prensa.* Buenos Aires

Archivo General de la República Argentina. Buenos Aires

Argentine Republic, Ministerio del Trabajo, Oficina Nacional de la Mujer, Dirección Nacional de Recursos Humanos. *Evolución de la mujer en las profesiones liberales en Argentina, años 1900-1965.* 2d ed. Buenos Aires: n.p., 1970.

Argentine Republic, Censo Escolar Nacional. Buenos Aires: 1884.

Argentine Republic, *The Argentine Civil Code.* Translated by Frank L. Joannini. 3 Vols. Boston: The Boston Book Company, 1917.

Asociación Cristiana Femenina. Buenos Aires

Biblioteca Juan B. Justo. Buenos Aires

Biblioteca Nacional. Buenos Aires

Cargos a la comisión directiva del Consejo Nacional de Mujeres. Buenos Aires: Talleres Gráficos Mentruyt, 1908.

Centro Femenino de Cultura Cívica documents.

Decreto de creación de la Sociedad de Beneficencia. Buenos Aires: January 2, 1823. In the Archivo General de la República Argentina.

Departamento Nacional de Trabajo: Boletín, December 31, 1907.

Departamento Nacional de Trabajo. Crónica Mensual VII. No. 81 (September, 1924): 1415-1425.

La escuela normal nacional Mary Olstine Graham. Obra escrito en celebración de su cincuentenario, 1888-1938. La Plata, 1938.

Estatutos de la Liga Nacional de Templanza de la República Argentina. Buenos Aires: n.p., 1922.

Federación de Mujeres Argentinas, Libro de Actas, 1945.

Federación de Asociaciónes Católicas de Empleadas, in the Biblioteca de la Asociación Cristiana Femenina. Buenos Aires.

In Memorium: Isabel King. Buenos Aires, 1904.

International Council of Women. Report of Transactions During the Third Quinquennial Meeting in Berlin. Boston: n.p., 1909.

Ley 12.341. Pan American Bulletin (June, 1937): 500-501.

Library of Congress. Washington D.C.

Perón, Eva. "Discurso de Eva Perón en el acto inaugural de la Asemblea Nacional del Movimiento Peronista Femenino." July 26, 1949.
_____ . "Habla a las trabajadores del país." Buenos Aires, 1949.
_____ . "Porque soy Peronista." 1949.

Primer Congreso Femenino Internacional de la República Argentina Buenos Aires: Alfa y Omega, 1910.

Report of the Inter-American Commission of Women to the 18th International Conference of American States on the Civil and Political Rights of Women, Lima, Peru (December 1938): 15.

República Argentina. Congreso, Camara de diputados Divorcio. Buenos Aires: El Comercio, 1902.

Rowe, L. S. "Educational Progress in the Argentine Republic and Chile" Report of the Commissioner of Education for the year ending June 30, 1909. Government Printing Office, Washington D.C. 1909,: 323-362.

Sociedad de Beneficencia de la Capital. Memoria del año 1916. Buenos Aires: Talleres del Asilo de Huérfanos, 1917.

Tercer Censo Nacional de la República Argentina. 1914.

Unión Argentina de Mujeres. "Merecemos las mujeres Argentina este agravio? Proyecto absurdo de Reforma del Código Civil." Buenos Aires, 1937.

_____ . *Memoria, 1936-38, Buenos Aires, 1938.*

Journals

Boletín Mensual del Museo Social Argentino, 1910-1930.

Caras y Caretas, 1910-1930.

Equal Rights

El Hogar, 1920-1950.

The International Women's News

El Normalista, 1899-1903.

The Pan American Magazine

Revista del Consejo Nacional de Mujeres de la República Argentina, 1900-1910.

Unión y Labor, 1910-15.

Vida Femenina

Woman Citizen, 1918-1926.

The Woman's Journal

Newspapers

Buenos Aires Herald (Buenos Aires)

El Día (Montevideo)

La Nación (Buenos Aires)

La Prensa (Buenos Aires)

La Razón (Buenos Aires)

La Vanguardia (Buenos Aires)

New York Times (New York)

Interviews

The Board of the Argentine branch of the International Federation of University Women, August 16, 1977.

The Board of the Consejo Nacional de Mujeres de la República Argentina, August 4, 1977.

Alicia Moreau de Justo, July-August, 1977.

Jorgelina Lozada, August, 1977.

Elena Bergman, August, 1977.

Unpublished Works

Akridge, Sharon A. Holenbeck. "Cinderella from the Pampas: María Eva Duarte de Perón, Argentine First Lady, 1919-1952." Dissertation, University of California, 1976.

Carlson, Marifran. "Feminism and Reform: A History of the Argentine Feminist Movement to 1926." Dissertation, University of Chicago, 1983.

Chaney, Elsa. "Women in Latin American Politics: The Case of Peru and Chile." Dissertation, University of Wisconsin, 1971.

Gerassi, Marysa. "Argentine Nationalism of the Right: The History of an Ideological Development." Dissertation, Columbia University, 1964.

Hall, Robert King. "The Secondary School in Argentina." Dissertation, University of Chicago, 1936.

Hernando, Diana. "Casa y Familia: Spatial Biographies in 19th Century Buenos Aires." Dissertation, University of California, 1973.

Hollander, Nancy Caro. "Women in the Political Economy of Argentina." Dissertation, University of California, 1974.

Lavrin, Asunción. "South American Feminists as Social Redeemers and Social Pioneers: Chile, Argentina, and Uruguay, 1900-1940. Manuscript.

Little, Cynthia Jeffress. "The Society of Beneficence in Buenos Aires, 1823-1900." Dissertation, Temple University, 1980.

López, Elvira. "El movimiento feminista." Dissertation, University of Buenos Aires, 1901.

McGee, Sandra F. "The Catholic Church, Work, and Womanhood, 1890-1930." Unpublished manuscript.
———. "The Social Origins of Counterrevolution in Argentina: 1900-1932." Dissertation, University of Florida, 1979.

Mirelman, Victor Alberto. "The Jews in Argentina, 1890-1930: Assimilation and Particularism." Dissertation, Columbia University, 1974.

Paul, Catharine Manny. "Amanda Labarca H.: Educator to the Women of Chile." Dissertation, New York University, 1967.

Percas, Helen. "Women Poets of Argentina, 1810-1950." Dissertation, Columbia University, 1955.

Schutter, H. "The Development of Education in Argentina, Chile, and Uruguary." Dissertation, University of Chicago, 1943.

Smith, Edmund Oscar. "Argentina and the Problem of Hemispheric Solidarity." Dissertation, University of Chicago, 1950.

Sweeney, Judy. "Immigrant Women in Argentina, 1890-1914." Master's thesis, University of California, 1977.

Weinstein, Donald. "Juan B. Justo: An Argentine Socialist." Dissertation, City University of New York, 1974.

Yoast, Richard A. "The Development of Argentine Anarchism: A Socio-Ideological Analysis." Dissertation, University of Wisconsin, 1975.

Index

This index includes references to people, cities, provinces, organizations, governmental bodies, institutions, documents, newspapers, books, laws, treaties and movements. References to the city of Buenos Aires or to the Catholic Church occur too frequently within the text to be included.